Computer Information Systems
Select Case Studies

Thomas L. Buck, Ph.D.

McGraw-Hill
Higher Education

New York   Chicago   San Francisco   Lisbon   London   Madrid   M
Milan   New Delhi   San Juan   Seoul   Singapore   Sydney   To

Library of Congress Cataloging-in-Publication Data

Buck, Thomas
     Computer Information Systems, Select Case Studies / by Thomas Buck.
         p.   cm.
     Includes bibliographical references (p.).
     ISBN-13: 978-0-9843779-2-3
     1.   Computer science – Information systems – United States.   I. Title: Computer Information
        Systems II. Title: Select Case Studies

AMII.C35   2016   923468

2   3   4   5   6   7   8   9   0   DSH/DSH   0   1   0   9   8

ISBN-13: 978-0-9843779-2-3
ISBN-10: 0-9843779-2-1

Cover and interior design by Thomas Buck

McGraw-Hill books are available at special quantity discounts to use as premiums and sales promotions, or use in higher education programs. For more information, please write to the Director of Higher Education Sales, Professional Publishing, McGraw-Hill, Two Penn Plaza, New York, NY 10121-2298. Or contact your local bookstore.

This book is printed on acid-free paper.

DEDICATION

This book is dedicated to following great
Information Systems students:

Alyssa Anderson
Daniel Blasena
Joleen Brandell
Donovan Chock
Emily Franklin
Patrick Gillespie
Meagan Krey
Steven Mueggenberg
Evan Mumbleu
Karli Niemann
Allison Raich
Zhiyu Yang

Thanks of giving me the material
For these Case Studies,
Even if you didn't appreciate them,
Or my sushi,
At the time.

CONTENTS

Foreword   i

Acknowledgements   iii

I. Excellent Sushi Eatery Case Series

Case 1 – Cost Benefit Analysis   1
Case 2 – Data Retrieval using SQL   9
Case 3 – Data Analysis with Pivot Tables   11

II. Collaborative Analysis and Presentation Case Studies

Case 4 - Occupational Employment Analysis   13
Case 5 – Business Process Design   17
Case 6 – Database Development and Management   19
Case 7 – Strategic Planning   21

III. Sushi Heights Case Series

Case 8 – Data and Process Modeling   29
Case 9 – Mission Statement   31
Case 10 – Information System Development   35
Case 11 – Data and Process Modeling   37
Case 12 – Object Modeling   39
Case 13 – Development Strategies   41
Case 14 – System Architecture   43
Case 15 – Systems Implementation   45

IV. Historical Business Case Studies and Activities

Case 16 – Amazon.com   47
Case 17 – Wal-Mart.com   55
Case 18 – Nintendo   59

Appendix A: Strategic Planning Examples and Worksheets   65

Computer Information Systems Glossary   97

Bibliography   125

About the Author   129

FOREWORD

These case studies are part of an on-going curriculum and simulations development project between the College of Saint Scholastica's School of Business and Technology (SBT) and Learning-Games.net (www.learningames.net). In general, these case studies are designed to help students explore the field of business systems analysis through case simulations and role-playing game (RPG) scenarios in combination with using a queueing theory model and both continuous, as well as discrete-event simulations. The related RPG scenarios still under development focus on real-life systems found in restaurant business performance and management systems. Through the case studies presented in this collection, students will explore mission critical systems commonly found in the modern, competitive restaurant industry. This simulation is also designed to teach and explore systems thinking and best practices through operations research modeling methods and solution algorithms in optimization, simulation, scheduling, and related areas.

Collaboration during the design and development processes of the case studies in this book, as well as their related simulations and RPGs, was twofold, on one side meetings, presentations and surveys were held with departments, faculty and staff from the SBT, Psychology, Health Information Management and Sandbulte Center to gain ideas for content and direction in the game development process. On the other side, a team of students with a variety of backgrounds was assembled to help in the final steps of development, and to review the case studies' content before curricular integration. Below is a partial list of the college of St. Scholastica students (and their majors) who, as of Spring 2016, have worked, and are currently working on this project:

- Alyssa Anderson (Health Information Management)
- Daniel Blasena (Computer Information Systems)
- Joleen Brandell (Health Information Management)
- Donovan Chock (Economics)
- Emily Franklin (Marketing)
- Patrick Gillespie (Health Information Management)
- Meagan Krey (Health Information Management)
- Steven Mueggenberg (Computer Information Systems)
- Evan Mumbleu (Computer Information Systems)
- Karli Niemann (Computer Information Systems)
- Allison Raich (Health Information Management)
- Zhiyu Yang (Computer Information Systems)

Each case has a set of initial questions at the end. These should be taken as a starting point. The primary objective is always the last question, which ranges from producing flow charts and diagrams, to create a report that defines a plan for moving forward. One useful way to approach is to (1) Identify the primary problems and causes of those problems, (2) Define a clear plan for the next steps to be taken, and (3) Explain how the plan solves the problems and provides additional benefits.

Remember that business problems rarely have a single correct answer. There is al-ways room for creativity and innovation. Just make sure that your solution will actually solve the main problems. Also, think about the implications of any solutions. Will it cause more problems than it solves?

Virtually any MIS case could be solved with the simple statement that the firm needs more computers. However, a one-line statement is not a very useful plan. In any business setting, you not only have to find an answer, you must also persuade others (executives) that your answer is the best alternative. Additionally, a good solution will contain an implementation plan—perhaps with a timetable that delineates each step of the process.

THOMAS L BUCK

ACKNOWLEDGMENTS

I would like to express my gratitude to the people who made this book possible. In particular, I would like to thank my learning games team-mate, Dr. Rick Revoir, for his continued work and guidance in the study of management, leadership, and ethical decision making; to Dr. Brandon Olson for giving me the opportunity to author and compile this collection of case studies and learning exercises; to Dr. Valerie Worthington for her thoughtful direction and advice in developing the course that led to this work; to Dr. Yaron Golan, my publisher, for his keen insight and creative problem solving techniques; and special thanks to both Dr. Gerald V. Post, for sharing his MIS case studies, and to our mutual friend Dr. Takei Takahashi, my sensei, friend, and master sushi maker. And finally, as I have said many times before, my core thanks especially goes out to my truest friend, and personal Managing Editor, Andrea Novel Buck, who patiently and continuously paid attention to every single word in my text, made supportive contributions and suggestions, and still said she loved me when she was done.

CASE 1 - EXCELLENT SUSHI:
COST BENEFIT ANALYSIS

Introduction

During his junior year in college, Bill Norland was invited by his friend Tom Norland to go out for dinner to a new upscale sushi restaurant. Bill wasn't sure how much liked sushi, he primarily ate at the fast food shops around campus. He'd never been to a traditional Japanese restaurant before and did not know what to expect. Tom told him it was a step above what he'd had before, and since Tom had been enjoying Japanese cuisine for several years, he could show Bill what he'd been missing. Bill agreed to give it a try and one cool Friday afternoon in the fall, Bill and Tom drove over to the new restaurant. Bill was immediately surprised by the authentic decor with servers in traditional Japanese wear, sliding paneled doors, and tatami mat rooms where they ate while sitting on the floor. The challenging names on the menu made it difficult for Bill to keep everything in order, but as they continued through the various stages of the meal, Bill's comfort level with the food improved and he began to enjoy the subtle nuances in the food and Japanese etiquette. It was a fantastic experience and the start of a lifelong passion for Japanese culture and cuisine.

Bill graduated from college a short time later, and before finding a job, decided to take a year off and go to Japan to live and study its culture, foods and traditions. When he returned to the United States, he found a job on the west coast selling life insurance. The pay was good, and the job was stable and secure. His early interest in Japanese culture continued to grow as well, and he enjoyed studying Japanese food etiquette and preparation, and regularly stopping by the various local sushi establishments after work. When at home, he was spending his spare time researching anything and everything about Japanese society, culture, traditions, food and language, and started taking classes in Japanese cooking. Also, while in Japan, Bill had developed an interest in three specific types of Japanese restaurants, but he was never able to find one that perfectly matched his diverse likes for all three of the various dishes and environments in one place. Each type of restaurant had its own strengths and weaknesses. The most formal and expensive type of traditional restaurant that Bill sometimes visited was the ryoutei (料亭). At a ryoutei Bill not only ate an elaborate multi-course meal, was also entertained by the venue, the decor, the table settings, and occasionally a geisha or other performers. Bill especially liked how this type of traditional multi-course cuisine had its roots in the tea ceremony. Another favorite type of restaurant that Bill enjoyed was the kappou-ryouri-ya (割烹料理), still a traditional Japanese restaurant, but less formal and smaller than a ryoutei, with western style table-and-chair or counter seating. His third favorite type is called taishuu shokudou (大衆食堂) - an eatery for the masses to translate it literally. This was an inexpensive restaurant that served many kinds of Japanese food, as well as a mix of western-style Japanese cuisine (i.e. curry rice, California rolls, etc.).

One day Bill was talking about Japanese foods with a client who he had recently sold a life policy to, while listening to him talk the customer realized how passionate and knowledgeable Bill was about the subject and asked Bill if he had every thought of starting his own restaurant. The client knew an investor who might be willing to back a new company focused on traditional Japanese cuisine and entertainment, with an additional western twist. Bill met with the investor and decided to open a restaurant that would incorporate aspects from all three types of Japanese restaurants. They decided to name the new eating establishment the Excellent Sushi Eatery (ESE) and the restaurant would focus on selling both Japanese and western dishes of high quality with different dining rooms that followed the different venues ranging from ryoutei, using two small rooms with tatami-mats and floor seating, to the taishuu shokudou, with a main dining hall that had tables and chairs, as well as both Japanese and western cuisine.

Both Bill and his investor understood that no single food-service operation has universal appeal, and in reality they could never capture 100 percent of the market. They followed the old marketing adage, "when you try to please everyone, you end up pleasing no one." So they focused on the 10 percent of the restaurant market that dealt with traditional Japanese dining, and decided to forget about the rest.

ESE hired employees to help with food preparation, serving, accounting, entertainment, and take out sales. They quickly found a good location, and developed several unique dishes that would top the menu. In the first year of business, ESE was able to cultivate a strong base of regular patrons. Bill realized that his first year's success meant there was a market for his kind of restaurant, so he decided to expand aggressively. He had a superior product at a reasonable price.

The Problem

Bill recognized early on that the success of ESE would depend on the ability of his employees to work together in an integrated fashion providing exceptional customer service. In the beginning when ESE was a small restaurant with 14 employees, it was easy to provide outstanding customer service. However, as ESE grew during the next three years, it expanded its operations to 50 full-time employees, a catering and delivery service, a sushi supply import service and $50,000,000 in revenue, customer service declined, customer complaints increased, and cash flow suffered. Furthermore, the sales team for the delivery and catering service was growing increasingly frustrated because they were promising products to customers they couldn't consistently deliver with the highest quality in a timely fashion.

Your Task

When Bill first started the venture, he invested in some computer equipment and basic software to help track important information. He was a strong believer in using information systems technology, so he purchased separate software applications to help keep track of data for each of the key functional areas in his organization - accounting, sales, and inventory operations. While these software applications served each functional area well, they lacked integration and required significant manual intervention to perform routine business processes. For example, when the sales team submitted an order in its order tracking software application, the order had to be printed out and delivered to the catering/delivery and accounting departments for processing. The manual process was problematic and Bill felt it was one of the key reasons for the decline in customer service. Accordingly, he was considering buying an enterprise system like SAP (from the German software company - Systems, Applications and Products) to use throughout the organization.

Before proceeding with the project, Bill has asked you to analyze the economic feasibility of replacing his existing suite of applications with SAP. Bill would like to know if the benefits realized from implementing the new SAP system exceed the costs of buying, implementing and using the system. Therefore, you must carefully examine the cost and benefits of replacing the legacy system with SAP. To facilitate your analysis, create a Microsoft Excel workbook detailing the costs of purchasing, configuring, implementing, and supporting the system along with a list of the projected benefits and cost savings. Your analysis should take into account the time value of money and calculate the overall net present value of the costs and benefits assuming a 20-year lifespan of the new system. The present value of a future cash flow may be calculated using the following formula:

$$\text{Present Value Factor} = \frac{1}{(1+r)^t}$$

Where,

r = discount rate
t = time period in years

The Costs

System costs may be categorized as either implementation costs or maintenances costs. Implementation costs occur only once, during system acquisition and implementation at the beginning of the project, while maintenances costs continue every year as long as the system continues to be used. Assume all implementation costs occur in year 0 and maintenances costs remain constant over the entire 20-year life span of the system. The following table summarizes the implementation and maintenance costs associated with the project.

Implementation Costs	Dollar Amount
Software Licenses	$500,000
Hardware	$75,000
Network and Communications Upgrades	$25,000
Training	$25,000
Configuration and Implementation	$2,750,000

Table 1 Implementation Costs

Maintenance Costs	Dollar Amount
Software License Maintenance Fees	$80,000
New IT Employees (2 x 90,000)	$180,000

Table 2 Maintenance Costs

The Benefits

As a result of using the new system, ESE expects to reduce inventory holding costs of raw materials and finished goods as well as dramatically increase their sales yield, which is the number of sales quotes resulting in a sales order, due to increased customer satisfaction, faster response time, dynamic pricing, and more efficient procurement, production and fulfillment processes. Prior to using the system, 50% of sales quotes resulted in an order. Using the new system, it is expected that 60% of sales quotes will result in a sales order thereby increasing revenue 10%. Assuming average annual sales of $50,000,000 with an average profit margin of 15%, the new system is expected to contribute $750,000 annually to net income. In addition to increased sales and profits, ESE expects to eliminate the positions of four clerical workers who are responsible for the collection, storage and processing of the documents used to support the manual process.

The following table summarizes the recurring benefits associated with implementing the new system.

Benefits	Dollar Amount
Increased Profit Due to Increased Sales	$750,000
Reduced Inventory Holdings Costs	$250,000
Reduction in Clerical Workforce (4 x 55,000)	$220,000

Table 3 - Benefits

The Deliverables

Part 1— The Excel Workbook

Use Excel to create a workbook to perform a cost benefit analysis of the project. The workbook should use fixed and variable cell references where applicable to support rapid assessment of the business case under different assumptions for interest rates, benefits and costs. The workbook should contain the following worksheets.

Table of Contents

This worksheet should describe the purpose of the workbook, list and describe each worksheet in the workbook, indicate the date the workbook was last modified, and provide the name of the person who created the workbook.

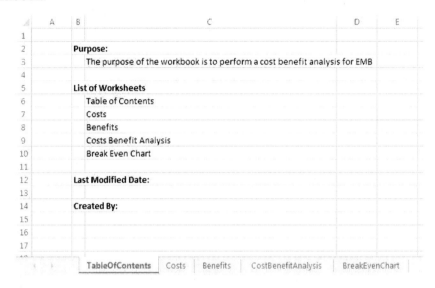

Figure 1 - Table of Contents

Costs

The "Costs" worksheet lists the implementation and maintenances costs for the project contained in Tables 1 and 2. Please calculate and display the sum for each cost category. (*Note: costs are negative.*)

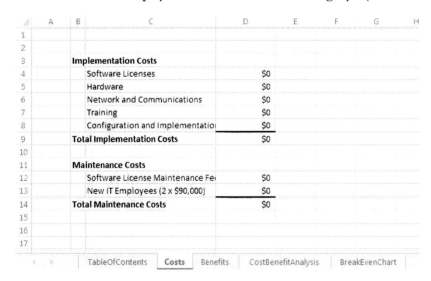

Figure 2 - Costs

Benefits

The "Benefits" worksheet lists the recurring benefits for the project contained in Table 3. You should also calculate and display the sum of all benefits.

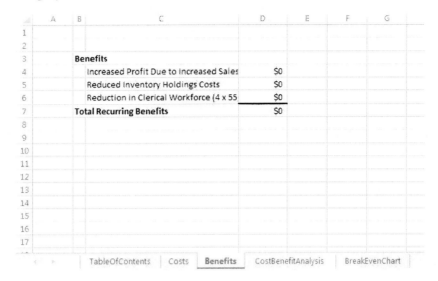

Figure 3 - Benefits

Cost Benefit Analysis

The "Cost Benefit Analysis" worksheet contains the discount rate, costs, benefits, present value factor, and the present value of costs and benefits for each year of the project. It should also include the Overall Net Present Value (NPV) for the proposed project, which is the net present value of all benefits minus the net present value of all costs. The following figure illustrates the layout of the "Cost Benefit Analysis" worksheet discussed above.

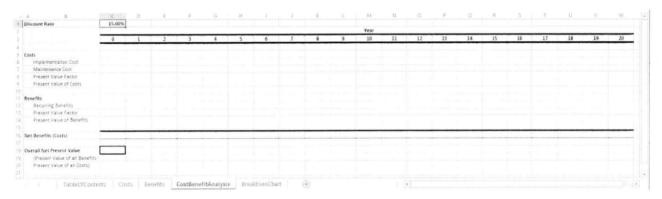

Figure 4 - Cost Benefit Analysis

Note: For "Cost Benefit Analysis" Formulas & Data see instructions and images below

1. Enter Discount Rate in cell C1
2. Because the Implementation Cost is only paid at the beginning of the first year, the Total Implementation Costs should only be listed under the first year (cell C6), then only $0s for all of the following years.
3. Because there are no Maintenance Costs in the first year, enter $0 in the first year (cell C7), then the Total Maintenance Costs should be entered in every following year.
4. & 7. For the Present Value Factor use the formula listed in the case study (or, 1 is divided by the quantity of 1 plus the Discount Rate to the power of the time period in years. In Excel, use the formula =1/(1+C1)^C$3 for all of the years starting at cell C8, and starting at cell

C13.

5. For the Present Value of Costs use the formula =(C6+C7)*C8, where it will take the combined values of Implementation and Maintenance multiplied by the Present Value Factor. Copy/Paste the formula to all the Year cells in that row.

6. Because the Recurring Benefits don't begin until after Implementation, enter $0 in the first year (cell C12), then the Total Recurring Benefits should be entered in every following year.

7. See Note 4.

8. For the present Value of Benefits use the formula =C12*C13, so it will display the Total Recurring Benefits multiplied by the Present Value Factor. Copy/Paste the formula to all the Year cells in that row.

9. For the Net Benefits (Costs) use the formula =C14+C9, so it will display the combined values of the Present Value of Costs with the Present Value of Benefits. Copy/Paste the formula to all the Year cells in that row.

10. For the Overall Net Present Value, sum the formula =SUM(C16:W16) to sum up all of the years' Net Benefits (Costs).

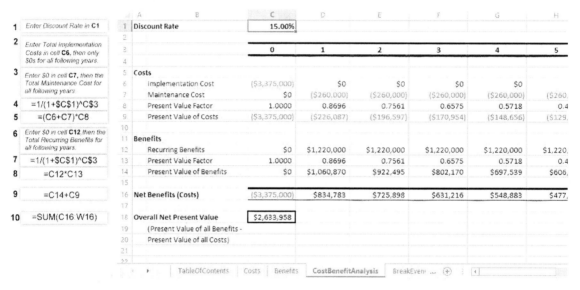

Figure 5 - Cost Benefit Analysis: Data & Formulas

Break Even Chart

Create a "Scatter with Smooth Lines" chart to graphically depict the break-even point for the project. Break-even occurs when the net present value of all costs equals the net present value of all benefits.

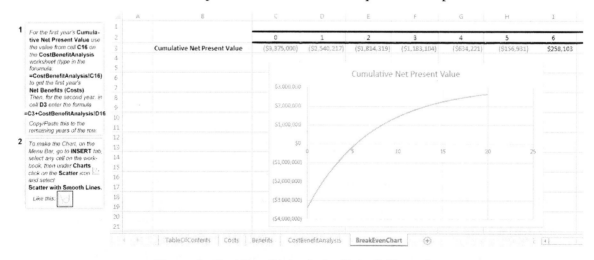

Figure 6 - Cost Benefit Analysis: Data & Formulas

Part 2— Questions to Answer using the Excel Workbook

Please answer the following questions using the workbook you created in Part 1. All questions should be answered in a separate Microsoft Word document.

1. Assume a discount rate of 15%. What is the overall net present value for the project? When will the project break-even? Should ESE move forward with the project and proceed with implementing SAP? Explain your answer.
2. Assume a discount rate of 30%. What is the overall net present value for the project? When will the project break-even? Should ESE move forward with the project and proceed with implementing SAP? Explain your answer.
3. Assume the recurring value of benefits due to increased sales was overly optimistic and net income due to increased sales is only $375,000 instead of $750,000. In addition, assume the benefits due to a reduction in inventory holding costs are only $50,000 instead of $250,000. Assuming a discount rate of 15%, what is the overall net present value for the project? When will the project break-even? Should ESE move forward with the project and proceed with implementing SAP? Explain your answer.
4. Assume the recurring value of benefits due to increased sales was overly optimistic and net income due to increased sales is only $375,000 instead of $750,000. In addition, assume the benefits due to a reduction in inventory holding costs are $50,000 instead of $250,000. At what discount rate is the project economically feasible? (Please note that the discount rate you calculate must include four decimal places of accuracy 12.3456%). Should ESE move forward with the project and proceed with implementing SAP? What are the implications of the changes to the economic feasibility of the project? Explain your answer.

CASE 2 - EXCELLENT SUSHI:
DATA RETRIEVAL USING SQL

Introduction

Please read the "Introduction" in Case 1 - Excellent Sushi Cost Benefit Analysis found on page 1 (required file: "http://www.tbuck.us/sushi_case_studies/case2and3emb.accdb").

Based on your thorough analysis of the cost and benefits of implementing an enterprise resource planning (ERP) system, Bill and his catering and sushi supplies sales team decided to move forward with a full-scale implementation of SAP (by the German software company - Systems, Applications and Products). Implementation lasted approximately 12 months and went smoothly for a project of such size, complexity, and scope.

The Problem

ESE has been using the new ERP system for approximately 12 months and they are thrilled with the initial gains in their catering service's productivity. Business processes have been formally defined and are routinely being followed, communication between departments has improved, delivery times have decreased, sales have increased, and employee morale has improved.

Now that the system configuration has stabilized, Bill would like to evaluate the performance of his organization using the transaction data being collected by SAP.

Your Task

ESE would like for you to perform an analysis of data contained in SAP using Microsoft Access. The SAP database administrator (DBA) has created a Microsoft Access data mart for you to use. The data mart is a small subset of the overall data contained in SAP and is available as a separate download file. The data mart contains sales orders for an entire year along with employee, customer and product information. To analyze the data, you will need to first understand relational databases and create queries to find and extract the data of interest.

Creating Queries using SQL

ESE would like for you to generate several queries using the SQL "Query Design" feature in MS Access. The queries are designed to provide an overview of the data stored in the data mart and techniques for answering specific questions about customers, products, and employees.

Query 1 - Employee List
Design a query to list all employees in the organization. The query should display the following information: employee ID, employee first name, employee last name, employee address, employee salary, department name, and region name. Execute the query and verify the output is correct. Once you are satisfied with the query, save the query as "Query1".

Query 2 - Sales Representative List

Design a query to list all sales people in the organization. The query should display the following information for the sales people in the organization: employee ID, sales rep first name, sales rep last name, sales rep address, sales rep salary, sales rep department name, sales rep region name. Execute the query and verify the output is correct. Once you are satisfied with the query, save the query as "Query2".

Query 3 - Customer List

Design a query to list all customers in alphabetical order by customer last name. The query should display the following information: customer ID, customer first name, customer last name, and customer birth date. Execute the query and verify the output is correct. Once you are satisfied with the query, save the query as "Query3".

Query 4 - Sales Orders by Quarter

Design a query to list all sales orders for the quarter you have been assigned to analyze sorted in ascending order by purchase order date. The query should display the following information: PO date, order ID, product ID, product description, quantity sold, and unit price. Execute the query and verify the output is correct. Once you are satisfied with the query, save the query as "Query4".

Query 5 - Finding a Sales Order

Construct a query to find the sales order with the ID 40000136856. The query should display the following information: PO Date, order ID, customer ID, customer first name, customer last name, product ID, product description, quantity sold, and unit price. Execute the query and verify the output is correct. Once you are satisfied with the query, save the query as "Query5".

Query 6 - Sales Orders for Export to Excel

Create a query to list all sales orders in ascending order by PO Date. The query should contain the following information: PO date, order ID, customer first name, customer last name, product ID, product description, quantity sold, unit price, sales rep first name, sales rep last name, and sales rep region name. Execute the query and verify the output is correct. Once you are satisfied with the query, save the query as "Query6".

Additional Information and Grading

The assignment is worth a total of 150 points and will be graded based on the following point allocation.

- 25 points for Query 1
- 25 points for Query 2
- 25 points for Query 3
- 25 points for Query 4
- 25 points for Query 5
- 25 points for Query 6

The Deliverables

The Access Database

Please turn in a copy of your Access database containing queries 1 through 6.

CASE 3 – EXCELLENT SUSHI: DATA ANALYSIS WITH PIVOT TABLES

Introduction

After completing your initial analysis of the data mart using SQL, Bill would you like you to perform a more detailed analysis using Microsoft Excel Pivot Tables. Pivot Tables are used to summarize large, complex data sets efficiently. Please read the "Introduction" in Case 1 - Excellent Sushi Cost Benefit Analysis found on page 1 (required file: "http://www.tbuck.us/sushi_case_studies/case2and3emb.accdb").

The Problem

The initial analysis performed using SQL was a good start, but it did not provide the level of detail Bill needs to make strategic and managerial decisions to improve the performance of his organization. He would like for you to conduct a more detailed analysis of ESEs (1) customers, (2) products, and (3) salespeople using Microsoft Excel Pivot Tables. Bill and ESE have requested your assistance with analyzing the data to identify patterns and trends and make recommendations that can be used to improve the overall performance of ESE.

Your Task

ESE would like for you to perform a detailed analysis of the data contained in SAP using Microsoft Excel Pivot Tables. Before creating the Pivot Tables, you must export the result set of query 6 in Case 2 to a Microsoft Excel Workbook. To export the query 6 result set, run query 6 by double clicking on it and export the results to Excel using the "Export to Excel" button on the "External Data" tab of Access. Save the exported data as "ESE Pivot Tables.xlsx". The pivot tables described below should be created from the data you export and all pivot tables should be contained in the same workbook (i.e. ESE Pivot Tables.xlsx") with each pivot table listed as a separate tab.

Creating Pivot Tables using Excel

Pivot Table 1- Customer Sales by Product

ESE would like to analyze the purchase patterns of customers. Specifically, ESE would like to know how much money each customer spent on various products. Create a pivot table to show the total sales dollar amount for each customer in descending order from high to low. The pivot table should list purchases by product type so that the columns display the amount of each product purchased along with the total amount each customer purchased. Which customer purchased the greatest dollar amount of products for the quarter? How much money did he or she spend? What product did he or she spend the most money on? What recommendations would you make to management based on this report? Save the pivot table as worksheet "Customers". (Hint: Customers should be displayed in rows and products should be displayed in columns. You should create a new column in the raw data set to compute the total sales amount prior to creating the pivot table. In addition, you should create a new column in the raw data set to display the customer's full name).

Pivot Table 2 - Products by Region

ESE would like to analyze the sales of products by geographic region. Create a pivot table to show the total sales dollar amount of each product in order from high to low with the product with the greatest amount listed first. The pivot table should list purchases by region name so that the column display the dollar amount of each product purchased by region name along with the total amount of each product sold. Which product had the highest sales dollar amount for the quarter? How much did the east region sell? What recommendations would you make to management based on this report? Save the pivot table as worksheet "ProductsByRegion".

Pivot Table 3 - Sales by Rep

EMB would like to analyze the sales of products by sales representative. Create a pivot chart to show the total sales by sales representative from high to low with the person selling the greatest dollar amount listed first. The pivot table should list sales representatives' names as rows and total amount sold as the only column and display the corresponding bar chart. Who sold the greatest dollar amount for the quarter? Who sold the least? What recommendations would you make to management based on this report? Save the pivot table as worksheet "Sales by Rep".

Pivot Table 4 - Product by Month

EMB would like to analyze the sales of products over time. Create a pivot chart to show the total sales by month for the Extreme Mountain Bike, The Extreme Plus Mountain Bike and the Extreme Ultra Mountain Bike. The Pivot Chart should display bar charts for each month indicating the dollar amount sold of each of the three products for a given month. Which month had the highest total bike sales? Which month had the lowest total bike sales? What recommendations would you make to management based on this report?

Save the pivot chart as worksheet "Products by Month". (Hint: Create a new column in the raw data set to compute the month prior to creating the pivot table.)

Additional Information and Grading

The assignment is worth a total of 100 points and will be graded based on the following point allocation.

- 25 points for Pivot Table 1 and questions
- 25 points for Pivot Table 2 and questions
- 25 points for Pivot Table 3 and questions
- 25 points for Pivot Table 4 and questions

The Deliverables

Excel Workbook

Submit a copy of your Excel workbook containing pivot tables 1 through 4. Answers to the discussion questions for each pivot table should be included directly in the Excel workbook.

CASE 4 - COLLABORATIVE GROUP PROJECT: OCCUPATIONAL EMPLOYMENT

Introduction

Working in a small group, you will analyze employment data for different occupations in the United States.

Please visit the online companion site for this book (http://www.tbuck.us/CIS_CaseStudies/) and download the Occupational Employment Statistics (OES) file. The OES file is published once a year by the US Federal Government and contains detailed employment statistics for every occupation in the US. Open the file in Microsoft Excel and create the following pivot tables.

Pivot Table 1 —Occupation by Salary and Size

Create a pivot table listing the average annual salary and total number of people employed in each occupation sorted in descending order from high to low by average annual salary. See the following figure for an example of what the pivot table should look like.

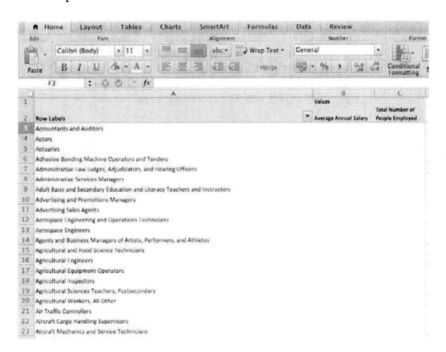

Figure 7 - Occupations by Salary and Size

Use the pivot table to answer the following questions and save the pivot table as PivotTable01.

1. What is the occupation with the highest average annual salary and how much does it pay?
2. What is the occupation with the lowest average annual salary and how much does it pay?
3. What does "#DIV/01" mean?
4. Which occupation employs the most people and how many people are employed in this occupation?

Pivot Table 2 — Occupations by Area

Create a pivot table with the average annual salary and total number of people employed for all occupations sorted in descending order by area name. See the following figure for an example of what the pivot table should look like.

Figure 8 - Occupations by Area

Use the pivot table to answer the following questions and save the pivot table as PivotTable02.

1. What is the area with the highest average annual salary?
2. What is the average annual salary for people working in the area with the highest average annual salary?
3. What area has the lowest average annual salary?
4. What is the average salary for people working in the area with the lowest average annual salary?
5. Which area employs the most people and how many people are employed in this area?

Pivot Table 3 — DFW Management Occupations

Create a Pivot Table with the average annual salary and total number of people employed in management occupations in the Duluth, MN-WI area sorted in descending order from high to low. (Hint: You need to filter the pivot table to only display occupations in Duluth and only display occupations beginning with the OCC Code 11). See the following figure for an example of what the pivot table should look like.

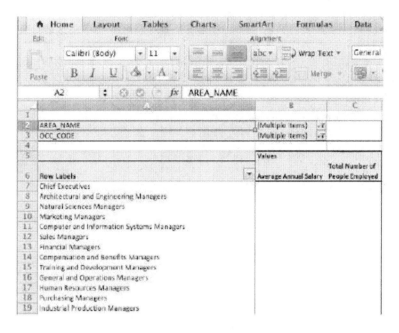

Figure 9 - Management Occupations

Use the pivot table to answer the following question and save the pivot table as PivotTable3.

1. What is the overall average salary for management occupations in the Duluth, MN-WI area?

Pivot Table 4 —Computer Systems Analysts

Create a Pivot Table with the average annual salary and total number of people employed as computer systems analysts in each area sorted in descending order by average annual salary.

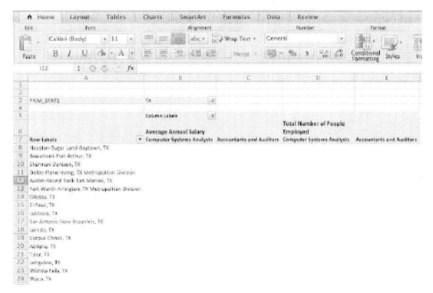

Figure 10 - Computer Systems Analyst Salary by Area

Use the Figure 5 pivot table to answer the following questions and save the pivot table as PivotTable4.

1. What is the area with the highest average annual salary for computer systems analysts?
2. How much do computer systems analysts earn in this area?
3. What is the area with the lowest average annual salary for computer systems analysts?
4. How much do computer systems analysts earn in this area?
5. Modify the pivot table to add an additional column with an occupation of your choosing. How does the pay of the occupation you selected compare to the pay of a computer systems analysts?

Additional Information and Grading

The assignment is worth a total of 100 points and will be graded based on the following point allocation.

- 20 points for Pivot Table 1 and questions
- 20 points for Pivot Table 2 and questions
- 20 points for Pivot Table 3 and questions
- 20 points for Pivot Table 4 and questions
- 20 points for Pivot Table 5 and questions

The Deliverables

Excel Workbook

Submit a copy of your Excel workbook containing pivot tables 1 through 5. Answers to the discussion questions for each pivot table should be included directly in the Excel workbook.

CASE 5 - COLLABORATIVE GROUP PROJECT: BUSINESS PROCESS DESIGN

Introduction

Working in a small group, you will formally analyze an organizational business and prepare and deliver a PowerPoint presentation of your analysis.

Your Task

Part 1- Business Process

Your presentation should start with a discussion of the business process you selected for analysis. You should define a primary input, a primary output and the steps to transform the input(s) into an output(s) along with the actor/person performing each step. List the steps and actors performing each step in a table.

Example: Processing payroll is an example of a business process. A primary input is the employee time card containing the number of hours worked during the pay period. A primary output is a check payable to the employee. A transformation process is the calculation of net pay (Gross pay less withholdings).

Process Step	Actor
1.Input hours worked	Employee
2.Approve hours worked	Supervisor
3.Calculate withholdings and net pay	Accounting
4.Output paycheck	Accounting

Table 4 - Process Steps and Actors

Part 2 - Process Model

Use the Internet to search for a company providing an information system to support the business process described in part 1. Create a process model that includes all interaction with the systems used to support the process and create a diagram of the process using Business Process Modeling Notation (BMPN). You will need Microsoft PowerPoint to create the process model.

Example: Continuing the example from above, QuickBooks Payroll from Intuit is an information system capable of processing payroll. The software can be installed on a single PC running Microsoft Windows and is designed primarily for small business owners to process payroll. The process model would list the sequence of activities from beginning to end. An example will be provided in class.

<u>Part 3 - Metrics</u>

Define at least 3 metrics to assess the performance of your process model. Define each metric and describe how each metric will improve the management of the business process.

- Number of payroll errors
- Time to process payroll
- Actor/User satisfaction

Additional Information and Grading

The assignment is worth a total of 100 points and will be graded based on the following point allocation.

- 30 points for part 1
- 30 points for part 2
- 30 points for part 3
- 10 points for the *questions* you ask other group presenters

The Deliverables

PowerPoint Presentation
Submit a copy of your PowerPoint presentation containing parts 1 through 3. The discussion questions for other group presenters should be included directly in the PowerPoint file as a separate slide.

CASE 6 - COLLABORATIVE GROUP PROJECT: THE FRESHMEN APP PACK

Introduction

You have been hired by UT Dallas as a systems analyst to help design a "Freshmen App Pack" consisting of a collection of smartphone applications for UT Dallas freshmen. The purpose of the App Pack is to help freshmen manage the transition to college. The smartphone applications included in your App Pack must provide value in some way to college freshmen and may address any day-to-day aspect of a freshmen's life (social, classroom, entertainment, etc.). The applications you select should be applications that have already been developed and published to the iTunes App Store. To view a list of available apps, download a copy of iTunes and click on "Store" then "App Store".

Your Task

Your group will develop and deliver a PowerPoint presentation covering the topics listed below.

Part 1 - Define App Pack Goals

List the goal(s) of your app pack summarizing the overall purpose. This should be done in a couple of sentences. You may choose any goal you want as long as it helps freshmen in their transition to college. For example, the goal of your app pack might be to help freshmen find and attend live local music performances.

Part 2 - Define App Pack Scope and Requirements

Define and list the major capabilities to be provided by your app pack. For example, major capabilities of your app might include the following:

1. Provide the ability to search for performances based on geographic location
2. Provide directions to and from performance venues
3. Provide an ability to listen to samples of live music performances
4. Provide an ability to read and write reviews of local live performances

Part 3 - List and Describe the Apps in the App Pack

Briefly describe each app you identified to satisfy the requirements listed in part 2. In addition, the requirement(s) each app satisfies should be clearly stated. Continuing the example from above, StubHub, AT&T Navigator, Pandora, and Facebook App provide the capabilities listed above of searching for performances, getting directions, listening to music samples and reading and writing reviews of performances. If possible, include screen shots of the apps.

Additional Information and Grading

The assignment is worth a total of 100 points and will be graded based on the following point allocation.

- 30 points for part 1
- 30 points for part 2
- 30 points for part 3
- 10 points for the questions you ask other group presenters

The Deliverables

PowerPoint Presentation

Submit a copy of your PowerPoint presentation containing parts 1 through 3. The discussion questions for other group presenters should be included directly in the PowerPoint file as a separate slide.

CASE 7 - COLLABORATIVE GROUP PROJECT: STRATEGIC PLANNING

Introduction

Strategic planning is often defined as the formal, disciplined process designed to help an organization identify and maintain an optimal alignment with the most important elements of its environment (Rowley, 1996). The result of the strategic planning process is a strategic plan.

Your Task

You will write a strategic plan (750-1000 words, or 4-5 pages; see Examples in Appendix A) for an Information Technologies department. You may base the plan on one of the businesses discussed in previous case studies, your current organization, or a previous organization that you have worked for.

Strategic Plan Requirements

The plan should include the following sections:

1. A description of the organization that you are basing the strategic plan on. This will include the organizational structure of the IT Department (i.e. Centralized or decentralized).
2. The mission or vision for the IT department
3. A list of goals or action plans for the upcoming year. A goal has three components:
4. A description of the project or action item and how it will lead to the achievement of the mission or vision of the IT department. In other words, why is it important to the organization.
5. A target completion date
6. An individual or individuals who are responsible for its completion
7. In the context of IT, there should be relevant goals and action items for each component, including the following (you can organize them however you wish):

   - data
   - hardware
   - software
   - network
   - security
   - Internet/web
   - reporting

Overview of Strategic Planning

A strategic plan is to tool that helps determine, map and define the direction and scope of the organization over the longer term, and is usually reviewed on a 3 or 5 year basis through a process. Strategic planning is the process of:

- Clarifying what the organization is about
- Deciding what is and is not a priority for the use of resources
- Analyzing the internal and external environment
- Considering how best to deal with upcoming changes and transitions
- Setting out a clear direction
- Setting concrete goals for the future

Strategic planning involves looking at the organization as a complete entity and is concerned with its long term development. This involves looking at what the organization was set up to do, where the organization is now, determining where you want to get to, and mapping how to get there.

The strategic plan should be summarized in a written document to ensure that all concerned are clear regarding the aims and objectives the organization is working towards. If the organization is a charity, the strategic plan must take account of the charity's purposes and public benefit requirement to ensure that the plan delivers what the charity was set up to do.

Development of a Strategic Plan

Strategic planning involves looking at the organization as a complete entity and is concerned with its long term development.

Developing the plan is a process that may involve discussion with a number of different stakeholder groups and should take place over a period of time. Whilst it is important to document your plan in written form to provide consistent guidance and a reference point for the organization, this should remain an active process. Your plans should be regularly reviewed to ensure that you are able to anticipate and adapt to challenges and changes in the internal and external environment.

There are a number of key stages in developing your strategic plan:

1. Determine who should be involved in the process and at what stage
2. Analyze where the organization is now
3. Discuss where the organization wants to be
4. Determine how the organization is going to get there
5. Produce a written strategic plan
6. Monitor and review your strategic plan

Stage 1

The first stage in development of a strategic plan for the organization involves determining who needs to be involved in the planning process.

The IT Department needs to decide who should be involved in the strategic planning process. Generally, it should involve as appropriate:

- Those who will be implementing the plan
- Those who will be affected
- Those who will monitor its implementation
- Others who can contribute to its development

COMPUTER INFORMATION SYSTEMS

When the IT Department has decided who will be involved, it is necessary to decide at what level and how different stakeholders will contribute to the organizations planning for the future. There are many different ways stakeholders can be involved, such as:

- An open day with a number of workshops
- A series of consultation meetings with specific groups
- A call for written submissions
- A questionnaire
- A steering group made up of a range of stakeholders

A combination of these approaches is likely to ensure that all groups/stakeholders have a say in developing the strategic plan.

Stage 2

Those involved in the strategic planning process must start with reviewing the present circumstances and characteristics of the IT Department. In order to plan for the future, you first need to reach a common understanding of the present circumstances. To answer this question you will need to focus discussions on two key areas:

     I. Analyzing the external and internal environment
     II. Reviewing/Developing the IT vision, mission and values

I. Analyzing the External and Internal Environment

Strategic planning is about having a clear direction to steer towards but also being able to respond to changes as necessary. To do this your department needs to have information about the challenges, opportunities and future trends, inside and outside. So whether the IT Department is just starting up or is already established, the first step in the planning process is to assess the external and internal position of an organization. A SWOT analysis is commonly used to identify.

S - Strengths (internal)
W - Weaknesses (internal)
O - Opportunities (external)
T - Threats (external)

Strengths and weaknesses primarily focus within the department. Opportunities and threats are primarily outside the department. This analysis of the environment allows the IT Department to take this into account when planning for its future.

SWOT Analysis of your IT Department (example)

STRENGTHS - What the organization is good at and is doing well

    Action on immediate systems issues and single user troubleshooting
    User training courses very popular
    Good support and back-up for staff and volunteers

WEAKNESSES - What the organization is not good at and which are not going well

> Accessing funding from a wider variety of sources
> Prioritizing work
> Evaluating regularly

OPPORTUNITIES - The events and trends that are favorable to the organization

> Introduction of Community Planning
> More tenders available for local work

THREATS - The trends or events that are unfavorable to the organization

> Reduced public sector funding
> Changes to benefits systems

Sample worksheets for conducting a SWOT Analysis can be found in Appendix A.

II. Reviewing the IT Department's vision, mission and values

Your SWOT analysis will provide key information on needs, priorities, problems and opportunities. On the basis of the needs identified, your department may need to redefine (or define) its vision, mission and values statement. These statements reflect what the IT plans or aims to do over the next 3 to 5 years. It is really important that each element of the SWOT analysis is used to consider what the future priorities for the IT Department should be. Appendix A has three worksheets specifically designed to help in the redefining (or defining) of the IT Department's vision statement, mission statement, and organizational values.

Stage 3

Having reviewed your current situation and the challenges and changes which will affect your future development, the next stage in strategic planning is to come to a common agreement regarding what the future should look like. To answer this question you will need to clarify:

- IT priorities for the next 3 to 5 years;
- IT strategic aims (long-term goals); and
- How these will help achieve your mission.

Your priorities for the coming period

Identify and agree your main priorities (e.g. services and key areas of work) for the period of the strategic plan (usually 3 or 5 years). These priority areas should emerge from your SWOT analysis of your internal and external environment and their effect on your organization's future.

Strategic Aims

Identify and write strategic aims (goals) for the organization. Strategic aims are broad statements of what the organization hopes to achieve.

The IT strategic aims should:

- Help achieve your mission
- Be limited in numbers (4 to 10)
- Show clear direction
- Be measurable.

Appendix A has three worksheets specifically designed to help in the redefining (or defining) of the IT Department's strategic aims.

Stage 4

The next step in developing a strategic plan is to work out how to get from where the department is, at present, to where it wants to be in the future. Creating a roadmap for achieving the strategic objectives will involve the IT Department in:

- Setting objectives
- Resourcing the IT Department
- Agreeing or approving operational/work plans
- Ensuring appropriate systems and structures are in place

Setting Objectives

Your objectives outline how each aim will be achieved. They should be SMART:

S - Specific
M - Measurable
A - Achievable
R - Realistic
T - Timebound

Your SMART objectives will guide the organization on:

- What will change or be achieved? What impact do you want to make?
- In what way? By how much?
- When? By what date?

Your objectives must relate to the strategic aims. It is important to check at this stage that all factors, internal and external, which have a bearing on the objectives set for the future work have been taken into account. In Appendix A there is a worksheet for developing strategic objectives.

Resourcing the Organization

The IT Department and those involved in the planning process must take into account the resource implications of the plans. They must review what is possible within the organization's available resources and where or how additional resources could be procured. This may also highlight gaps in resources such as people required, equipment, or facilities, as well as financial limitations.

Agreeing Operational / Work Plans

The operational plan outlines the day-to-day program of work based on the aims and practices of the strategic plan. It may also be referred to as an "action plan", "work plan" or "implementation plan". This is normally done annually. The detail of the operational plan is linked to each objective of the IT Department and will provide information on:

- What will be done
- Who is responsible
- How it will be done
- With what resources:
  - Human - volunteers, staff, users, management
  - Physical - premises, location, equipment
  - Financial
- What success will look like or what targets should be reached
- How will impact be measured?

Ensuring Appropriate Systems and Structures

The organization needs to ensure that the necessary structures are in place to facilitate the implementation of its aims and objectives. The structures include the shape of the organization, the roles within it, the rules, procedures and policies, and management structures.

They should define who is accountable, to whom and for what. The department may need to plan for changes and developments in its existing structure as a result of its future priorities and aims. This may involve reviewing, for example:

- How staff and management are organized
- Resources such as money, equipment, premises
- Training requirements.
- How outcome measurement will be built in from the beginning of the work

---

Stage 5

Every organization should have a written plan for its future development, documenting the outcomes of the strategic planning process. Your plan should outline how the department plans to achieve its aims and objectives. It should demonstrate that there is effective control and management of the department by including a governance section with examples of controls.

It is important that your written plan is 'bought into' by your full department by involving people at the earliest stages and is not merely a paper exercise. There are a range of departments that can guide you in deciding what type of written plan is most relevant for your department's needs, and can assist you in developing such plans.

The extent and detail of your written plan will depend on the nature and size of your group or department, but the following are headings to guide you in structuring your strategic/business plan:

Executive Summary

A summary of the plan; you may wish to make this summary something you can promote outside the department, to build support and keep stakeholders informed.

Introduction

The purpose of the plan; background about where the IT Department is in its development; brief statistics about the numbers of staff/volunteers; a description of service users (snapshot).

Purpose

Cover the (new) mission, vision and values for the department – this is the backdrop for the plan; say how you use these important statements.

Internal Appraisal

Provide a concise review of the current health of the department; summarize the strengths and weaknesses and their implications; make sure you cover key achievements in the previous period. Ensure you provide an overview of governance arrangements.

Future Potential

Outline what the challenges are for the future (external opportunities, threats, other player potential, stakeholder needs etc.).

Strategic Aims and Priorities For Change for the Next Three Years

Cover the main areas of work the department needs to focus on for the next three years. Each objective should have key tasks and outcomes associated with it – from which you can develop annual goals and teams and individuals can develop their work plans.

Delivering the Plan (Resources and Timetable)

This is where you need to be convincing about the department's ability to resource the plan. Attach a budget and a 'timeline' to show when and how the strategic objectives will be met and how they will be managed (covering all the main areas of work of the department).

Stage 6

The final step in any planning process is to monitor and evaluate progress. The same way as you check the signposts along a road when completing a journey, it is similarly important to check that development is on track.

The IT Department should use reports against its annual operational plans to review progress towards meeting the strategic aims and objectives. Therefore, they must ensure that whoever is doing the work is keeping appropriate records so that progress can be assessed. This will involve, at the implementation stage of your plan, being clear what systems and structures are required. The things you decide to measure will give an indication of how well you're doing, hence, the name indicators or performance measures.

Before completing your plan, you need to agree how and when it will be monitored and reviewed and what information the IT Department needs to receive in order to review progress. When reviewing progress towards achieving the strategic aims and objectives, the IT Department should:

- Ensure that activities are kept within the parameters of the agreed strategic aims and objectives;
- Ensure that activities are consistent with department's vision, mission and values;
- If the department is a charity, use the information collected to show the public benefit the charity is having
- Keep under review internal and external changes which may require adjustments to the department's strategy or affect their ability to achieve their objectives.

Additional Information and Grading

The assignment is worth a total of 200 points and will be graded based on the following point allocation.

- 80 points for SWOT and Development Worksheets
- 80 points for Strategic Plan Report
- 30 points for PowerPoint Presentation
- 10 points for the *questions* you ask other group presenters

The Deliverables

Completed Worksheets
- Stage 2 - SWOT analysis questionnaire
- Stage 2 - SWOT Analysis Worksheet
- Stage 2 - Developing Department Values Worksheet
- Stage 2 - Developing a Mission Statement Worksheet
- Stage 2 - Developing a Vision Statement Worksheet
- Stage 3 - Priorities and Strategic Aims Worksheet
- Stage 3 - Example Strategic Aims
- Stages 3 & 4 - Strategic Objectives Worksheet

Written Strategic Plan
Submit a copy of your completed strategic plan in a Word Document

PowerPoint Presentation
Submit a copy of your PowerPoint presentation containing overviews and a summary of your work in the Development Stages 1 through 6, as well as your finished Strategic Plan.

CASE 8 – SUSHI HEIGHTS: IT JOB INTERVIEW

Introduction

You have an interview for an IT/Systems Analyst position with the Sushi Heights Corporation which uses structured analysis and relies heavily on modeling, prototyping, and CASE tools. As you prepare for your interview you decide to review some IT terms and concepts. You want to be ready for the interview, read the job description below, and answer the following IT questions.

Sushi Heights – Systems Analyst

Position Overview:

You may know us as a company with great food. You may also know us from Fortune's "10,000 Best Companies to Work For" list. What you may not know is we are a company driven by technology.

As the Systems Analyst you will have a seat at the table and play an integral role in influencing the design and decisions regarding our technologies, process, and innovation. You will no longer be stuck in a box; you will be an agent of change and a part of the solution. You will interact company-wide with multiple departments including Finance, Human Resources, Marketing, Legal, and Operations.

Reporting to the Sr. Manager of Corporate Systems, you will be on a team of six within an IT department of forty. You will support our corporate office, located in Calabasas Hills including over three hundred staff members.

Duties:

- Provide world-class technical support optimizing and streamlining: ERP (Enterprise Resource Planning), SaaS and commercial off-the-shelf applications for our Finance, Human Resources and Payroll departments.
- Install, support, and extend packaged applications, including the design and development of business process automations.
- Analyze business requirements to design solutions that will enhance ERP, SaaS and off-the-shelf applications.
- Use Transact-SQL to gather structured data to create reports, interfaces and ad-hoc analysis. This includes the creation of tables, indexes, stored procedures and views as needed.
- Quality assurance that includes unit, systems, integration and user acceptance testing.
- Assist with upgrades and the implementation of new solutions for ERP, SaaS and off-the-shelf applications.
- Grow your skills by attending workshops and conferences in an effort to stay current on emerging technology.

About Us:

Recognized as one of the FORTUNE "10,000 Best Companies to Work For" in 2015, The Sushi Heights Incorporated operates more than 18 full-service, casual dining restaurants throughout the U.S. and Puerto Rico. Internationally, seven of The Sushi Heights restaurants operate under licensing agreements. Continuing on our path to becoming a Global Iconic Brand, we employ more than 350 staff members, 32 of whom work at the corporate support center in Calabasas Hills, CA

The Sushi Heights Incorporated is an Equal Opportunity and E-Verify Employer and provides reasonable accommodations consistent with its legal obligations; we do not provide work visa sponsorship.

Your Task

Research and Answer the following questions:

1. What are the differences between structured, O-O, and agile development methods? Which method do you think is best, and why?
2. What is a CASE tool and why is it important? What are two CASE tool examples?
3. What is business process modeling and how is it done?
4. What is prototyping and why is it important? What industries are likely to use prototyping?

Additional Information and Grading

The assignment is worth a total of 40 points and will be graded based on the following point allocation.

- 10 points for Task 1
- 10 points for Task 2
- 10 points for Task 3
- 10 points for Task 4

The Deliverables

Word Document
Submit your answers for Tasks 1 through 4 as a Word Document.

CASE 9 – KAHUNA SUSHI SUPPLY: MISSION STATEMENT

Introduction

One of Sushi Heights' northeast US suppliers is Kahuna Sushi Supply, a family-run business based in New Haven, Connecticut. The sushi company specializes in commercial sushi supplies and restaurant support products for commercial, and institutional clients in New England and Eastern New York. Kahuna Sushi Supply originated in response to the growth of the cities of Bridgeport and New Haven from the suburban spread from New York City. The business has grown to fourteen warehouse locations, each with several delivery trucks depending on the volume of sales at each location.

Background

With the stagnant population growth in Connecticut since 1980, Kahuna Sushi Supply made a concerted effort to expand their market into other areas in the region, first in Connecticut, and then in the broader New England region. The early efforts included increased advertising and an increase in the sales force, with an emphasis on cold calls to potential customers. This strategy proved to be a successful businesses model in the 1990s and early 2000s that allowed them to grow, but recently their growth has been flat. Getting new clients has been difficult in the down economy and existing clients are shopping for better prices.

In 2012, the next generation of Mushashi joined the company with the addition of Julia Mushashi as the vice president of Kahuna Sushi Supply. Julia, a graduate of the business school at the University of Connecticut, is full of ideas for bringing Kahuna Sushi Supply into the 21st century and expanding the customer base to the national arena. She and her father, Charles Mushashi, president of Kahuna Sushi Supply, have different ideas about the paths to follow to ensure the fiscal health of the company. Although both agree that the customer base needs expansion, they disagree on how large this expansion should be. Julia also wants to put an information system in place that can provide a seamless, efficient, and user-friendly environment for their business, with a Web-based component for customers to place and track orders.

Up until now, the sales and office staff has been using a text-based point of sales and warehouse management system for taking orders, putting together shipping and delivery lists, and generating billing information. Recently the financial department has moved to a software package that handles accounts payable and accounts receivable. This new package has expansion capabilities by purchasing additional modules from the vendor. Charles understands spreadsheets, but anything demonstrated to him beyond that has received a negative response because of his limited comfort level with technology. He is also concerned about the impact of an information system on his workforce, some of whom have been at the company longer than he has, and most of whom have limited knowledge of computers. Charles is in favor of adding additional salespeople and expanding the market down the eastern seaboard.

Julia wants to see Kahuna Sushi Supply moving toward an online presence and a national market. She is interested in exploring the possibility of reducing the traditional sales force and introducing a Web presence that provides information about products and allows potential customers to use online tools to build supply quotes and orders. Her vision is for large clients and janitorial service customers to use an online portal for electronic data interchange (EDI) for orders to replenish their inventory stock. She wants Kahuna Sushi Supply to use EDI with its suppliers, which will help the company use just-in-time inventory methods and realize savings from manufacturers and improve efficiencies in logistics.

Andrew McClean, the director of sales, is concerned about the direction that Julia is interested in exploring. He has been with the company for over thirty years, and supports Charles Mushashi's ideas for increasing sales by expanding the sales force and the geographical target area. He does acknowledge that there is support from sales people for the introduction of an information system, and that his hesitancy is influenced largely by his discomfort with technology. He also acknowledges that customers have expressed frustration with the time needed to get information about prices and track orders because they have to go through their sales representatives. Sales representatives establish close, personal relationships with their clients, determine the profit margins charged to clients, place orders, and provide most of the customer service.

Anna McNally, the director of finance, would like to see a more integrated solution for following orders from quotes through delivery and billing. She points out that with the multiple solutions currently being used for the various components of orders, errors can be introduced at several points of the process, whenever information moves from one process to another.

Martha Seymour, the director of operations, is happy with the current computerized order process, even though it was implemented many years ago and has not been updated in several years. She is concerned with the fact that orders, inventory, and new stock replenishments from manufacturers do not always match up. Sales people sometimes sell more product than what is currently on hand, and new stock shipments do not arrive in time to get delivered to customers by their need by date. The result of this has caused some customers to be unhappy due to the human errors. Martha does not want to see a change in the delivery process itself, but if the software they are using to synchronize the sales and logistics system can be updated to allow for automatic linking between sales, new stock orders, and delivery, she would be supportive.

Charles and Julia have decided to bring in a systems analyst to evaluate their business situation and whether or not implementing an IT solution for some or all of their business needs make sense. Charles has decided that he will have Julia be the main contact person for this because he does not have the background he feels is necessary to make informed decisions in a timely fashion. They hired Robert Hanover, a systems analyst who does a lot of work for small scale commercial supply companies.

IT System Analysis

Julia, Charles, Andrew, Anna, Martha, and Robert sit down to discuss the business, and most notably the areas that Julia feels could benefit most from an IT system.

Julia: Robert, I think that the most important issue for our company is coming up with a solution for the fragmented nature of the process that follows orders from placement to delivery. We currently have different solutions in place for quoting prices, taking orders, ordering stock, tracking the orders through the delivery process, and billing the customer. Each one of these sub-processes is separate and distinct, and much of the information that follows an order from start to finish has to be entered multiple times along the way. We have to come up with a solution that is more efficient for both the company and the customer.

Andrew: Well, you know that I am not technology-savvy, but I am hearing from my sales force that we need to be doing something. Sales reps are frustrated that customers can't easily check on orders, or get estimates, without working with the sales rep or someone at the home office. They are being told that many other companies provide them with the capability to check prices and check on orders themselves through some computer-based system. Customers seem to be much more self-sufficient and in more of a hurry now than they used to be. Our rep-dependent system is putting us at a disadvantage.

Anna: I'm quite happy with my new software that is handling accounts receivable and accounts payable. My concern right now is that billing still is being generated outside of this software and moving billing info over to accounts receivable requires several steps to prepare and export the information. Each step has the potential to introduce error because it is dependent on human intervention. Why can't we move this information over using an automated process that removes the human element and, therefore, the errors?

Martha: I'm in the same boat as Anna. I'm quite happy with my sales and delivery system, and I don't want to see that changed. My concern is the link between inventory and sales because of the potential for error to be introduced. I know that the vendor who sold us the point of sales system has called a couple of times about upgrades, but we have never pursued this. Perhaps this might be the time to find out more within the context of a new IS?

Charles: You all know where I stand on this. We built this company with good people, and I do not want to replace people with computers. Is that what would happen if we brought in one of these information systems? I want this company to continue to maintain strong, personal relationships with our clients and take care of our employees; even if that means that we grow a little less.

After the meeting, Julia asked Robert to put together in writing his impressions from the meeting. She is interested in formalizing the goals of the company, planning out how to meet these goals, and addressing some of the reservations that Charles and Andrew have about introducing an IS at Kahuna Sushi Supply. Robert begins to review his notes from the meeting to prepare a presentation for Julia.

Your Task

Review the Case Study and Answer the following questions:

1. Does a strong business case exist for developing an information system to support this sushi supply business? Explain your answer.
2. In a small- to medium-sized business, is it really important to use a structured approach for information systems development? Why or why not?
3. Based on the facts provided, draft a mission statement for Kahuna Sushi Supply. In your statement, consider all the stakeholders who might be affected by Kahuna Sushi Supply operations.
4. What internal and external factors might affect Kahuna Sushi Supply business success?

Additional Information and Grading

The assignment is worth a total of 40 points and will be graded based on the following point allocation.

- 10 points for Task 1
- 10 points for Task 2
- 20 points for Task 3 – Mission Statement
- 10 points for Task 4

The Deliverables

Written Mission Statement

Submit a copy of your completed Mission Statement (task 4), and your answers for Tasks 1, 2 and 4 as a Word Document.

CASE 10 – KAHUNA SUSHI SUPPLY: INFORMATION SYSTEM DEVELOPMENT

Introduction

One of Sushi Heights' northeast US suppliers is Kahuna Sushi Supply, a family-run business based in New Haven, Connecticut that specializes in commercial sushi supplies and business support products for commercial, industrial, and institutional clients. Only a few computerized operations are in the business. In an effort to become more efficient and profitable, the vice president, Julia Thompson, has hired a systems analyst, Robert Hanover.

Background

Julia and Robert have made progress in the development of a strategic plan for Kahuna Sushi Supply. Robert is anxious to define the requirements for the new system. He has gathered more information and has created the following organization chart for Kahuna Sushi Supply.

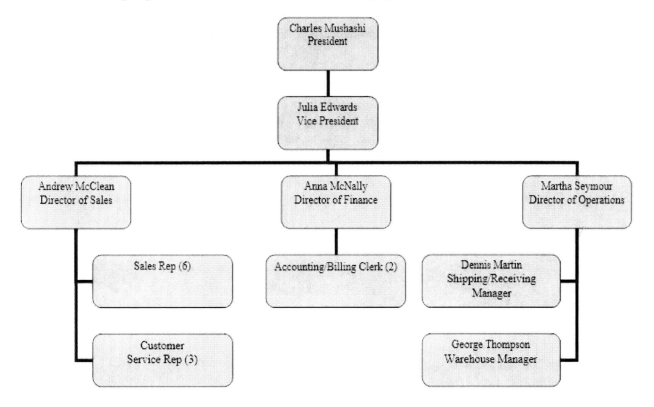

Figure 11 - Management Occupations

Robert: Julia, it's time to start moving on the system investigation. The mission statement is finalized and strategic planning is well underway. I can see that the directors are beginning to think about how their departments can benefit from better information management.

Julia: You're right! Andrew McClean found out that we lost a big order the other day because the customer was able to get the estimate much more quickly from a company in the Midwest because of their online presence. He's wondering just how many sales we are losing because of timeliness issues. I had Anna's group gather numbers for the directors about how many times our profit margin has been reduced because of human error somewhere along the order process. We are profitable, but could be more so by reducing error and becoming more competitive with timely information to our potential customers.

Robert: Andrew's area of sales is a logical place to start the investigation. I need to interview sales and customer service representatives to get an idea of the requirements for the new information system. What kind of information will we include? What do we want to get out? What processes need to be managed? What are our business needs?

Julia: This will take some time, and a lot of information needs to be gathered. You should make sure you spend some time with the accounting clerks too, because they fill in for customer service representatives.

Robert: I'm ready to get started!

Your Task

Review the Case Study and Answer the following questions:

1. Develop a fact-finding plan including interviews, documentation review, observation, questionnaires, sampling, and research.
2. Review the organizational model above and list the individuals you would like to interview. Prepare a list of objectives for each of the interviews you will conduct.
3. Prepare a list of specific questions for each individual you will interview.
4. Design a questionnaire that will go to a sample of Kahuna Sushi Supply customers to find out if they were satisfied with the sales and ordering process. Also, decide what sampling method you will use and explain the reason for your choice.

Additional Information and Grading

The assignment is worth a total of 50 points and will be graded based on the following point allocation.

- 10 points for Task 1
- 10 points for Task 2
- 10 points for Task 3
- 20 points for Task 4 – Customer Questionnaire

The Deliverables

Written Fact-finding Plan
Submit a copy of your completed fact-finding plan including a list of your targeted interview objectives and specific questions; completed customer questionnaire; and, your sampling and research strategies.

CASE 11 - SUSHI HEIGHTS:
DATA AND PROCESS MODELING

Introduction

Sushi Heights is considering the creation of a Sushi Delivery service where the customer can place an order, either online or via phone, and have the order delivered directly to them. To help in the process development the company is examining a number of different ordering and delivery services, both in the U.S. and Japan. As a Systems Analyst, you have been given the job of analyzing a successful ordering system used by a small take-out restaurant near the University of Colorado, Denver (UCD) campus.

Sakura Square Sushi is a small restaurant on Sakura Square Ave. Most of its customers are UCD students. In the current manual ordering system, the restaurant employees have to go through three different activities in order to process a sushi order. The first activity, called Receiving the order, consists in getting customers' information (such as name, phone number, and address), and getting orders' information (such as the amount of sushi, the type of sushi, and the specific ingredients needed to make the sushi). The same process also checks the availability of the ingredients needed before setting the status of the sushi order as "valid". When a sushi order is valid, the employee in charge of receiving the order provides the valid order information to the chefs who make the sushi. The second activity, making the sushi, consists in getting the ingredients needed and actually making the sushi. At the end of that process, the chefs have to update the manual file that keeps track of the ingredients. They also provide the drivers in charge of delivering the sushi with the (completed) status of the order. The final activity, delivering the sushi, done by the drivers consists in getting address and payment information from the employee in charge of Receiving the order, and actually delivering the sushi. The drivers provide the customers with a receipt and get payment.

Your Task

For this case simulation use Lucidchart (https://www.lucidchart.com/) to do the following:

1. Name all the processes to be found in the Data Flow Diagram of the system.
2. Name all the external entities to be found in the Data Flow Diagram of the system.
3. Name all the data stores to be found in the Data Flow Diagram of the system.
4. Draw the Data Flow Diagram for the new Sakura Square Sushi's ordering system.

Additional Information and Grading

The assignment is worth a total of 55 points and will be graded based on the following point allocation.

- 10 points for Task 1
- 10 points for Task 2
- 10 points for Task 3
- 25 points for the Task 4 - Data Flow Diagram

The Deliverables

Data and Process Modeling Diagrams
Submit text and your diagram in a Word Document.

CASE 12 - NIPPON SUSHI & SASHIMI SHACK: OBJECT MODELING

Introduction

The Nippon Sushi & Sashimi Shack is a family-owned business that operates on the Gulf Coast. The company already uses both financial and point-of-sale (POS) software, but has been unable to find a suitable system to manage its inventory and purchase orders. You are an independent consultant who has been hired to develop an inventory and order system for the company.

Background

Nippon Sushi purchases a variety of seafood (tuna, mackerel, shrimp, eel, crab, etc.) from local fishing boats and fresh vegetables from local farmers to make sushi and sashimi. Other food products are purchased from an Asian grocery wholesaler. Nippon Sushi sells its products through a variety of outlets, most notably its restaurant. The company sells prepackaged sushi and sashimi to supermarkets, hospitals, and other companies for resale. To ensure profitability, the company prices its products based on the estimated material cost that goes into producing them. Restaurant food is sold at cost plus 200 percent, wholesale orders are sold to retailers at cost plus 60 percent and smaller orders including catering events are sold at cost plus 100 percent. Due to the volatility in prices of seafood, menu prices are updated on a regular basis.

Currently, the company uses a journal to record its purchases and orders. Any employee can add, edit, or strike out a journal entry. When new seafood or vegetable products arrive, employees must record the type, total weight, and cost as a new journal entry. A spreadsheet is used to keep track of inventory totals. Wholesale and retail prices are manually calculated and entered into the POS software. Inventory is pulled out of stock on a first in, first out basis. As the business continues to grow, this system is becoming less viable. Some of the shortcomings include:

1. Employees sometimes make clerical mistakes or forget to record transactions.
2. When the inventory holds a particular type of seafood or produce that has been purchased at different times and costs, it is difficult to determine the correct cost bases and some older food is spoiling before getting sold because food preparers are taking out stock in the wrong order.
3. Sales prices have to be manually calculated, a process that can take a lot of time to complete.
4. You have completed the systems planning phase; the next step is to create an object-oriented model of the inventory and orders system.

Your Task

For this case simulation use Lucidchart (https://www.lucidchart.com/) to do the following:

1. Create a use case diagram for an inventory and order system.
2. Create a class diagram for classes you would expect to find in Nippon Sushi's system.
3. Create a sequence diagram for some aspect of the new system.
4. Create a state transition diagram that describes a changing state in the system

Additional Information and Grading

The assignment is worth a total of 100 points and will be graded based on the following point allocation.

- 25 points for the Task 1 - Use Case Diagram
- 25 points for the Task 2 - Class Diagram
- 25 points for the Task 3 - Sequence Diagram
- 25 points for the Task 4 - State Transition Diagram

The Deliverables

Object Modeling Diagrams
Submit copies of your diagrams 1 through 4 either as a .jpeg or Word Document.

CASE 13 - THE OCEAN SOUND CULINARY SUSHI COLLEGE: DEVELOPMENT STRATEGIES

Introduction

Ocean Sound College is a culinary sushi college located on the West Coast, and is a subsidiary of the Sushi Heights Corporation. You are the systems analyst assigned from the college IT department to conduct the systems analysis phase of the development of a new listing system for the school's housing office.

Background

Based on your earlier recommendations, the housing office decided to continue the systems development process for a new listing system.

Now, at the end of the systems analysis phase, you are ready to prepare a system requirements document and give a presentation to the housing office.

You must examine tangible costs and benefits to determine the economic feasibility of several alternatives. If the housing office decides to go ahead with the development process, the system can either be developed in-house or purchased as a vertical package and configured to meet the needs of the office.

Currently, housing listings are created by an employee at the housing office. While the demands on her time vary throughout the year, based on previous work logs kept by employees in the office you determine that the time spent maintaining the manual system (creating listing sheets for the various binders, copying, and filing listings in binders) by this employee works out to an average of 30 hours of overtime per month. The overtime cost of this employee is $25 per hour, including overhead.

Housing listings are pulled throughout the month, and all listings are reviewed once a month to delete those more than two months old. Currently, the once a month reviews are done by a student worker who spends 25 hours a month going through the 15 binders at the housing office, and pulling all old listings for review by a housing office staff member. This student is paid $12.50 per hour, including overhead. A new system would conduct this review automatically, and generate a list for review.

Your estimates indicate that the housing office can expect to have staff spend 4 hours a week performing maintenance, file backups, and updating of the new system, at $25 per hour.

The university has lost revenue on some of its rental properties, having them lie idle for a month because of listings pulled either erroneously by staff, or deliberately by people using the housing listing service. Estimates put the amount of lost revenue due to listing problems such as these at two percent of anticipated yearly rental receipts. In the current year, the anticipated rental receipts total $680,000. Annual increases of rent vary from year to year depending on market rates but the average increase is three percent per year.

Based on your research, you originally estimated that an in-house development project could be completed in about three weeks. This time estimate is based on 55 hours a week split between you and another analyst from the IT department. The IT department uses a charge-back rate of $40 per hour for work for other university departments. Three training sessions of four hours each will be required to train all staff in the new system. The charge-back cost of a training specialist from the IT department is $25 per hour. Training and technical support for the first year for the vertical software package is included in the initial price.

As an alternative to in-house development, a vertical software package is available for about $6,000, including an on-site day of training and technical support for the first year. If the department buys the package, it would take you about two weeks to install, configure, and test it, working full-time. The vendor provides free support during the first year of operation, but then the housing office must sign a technical support agreement at an annual cost of $750.

For both the in-house development and the vertical software package, the necessary hardware will cost about $3,500. Network upgrading, necessary for either option, has been estimated at $4,000 by the network operations team.

In your view, the useful life of the system will be about five years, including the year in which the system becomes operational.

Your Task

You scheduled a presentation to the housing office next week and you must submit a system requirements document during the presentation. .Prepare both the written documentation and the presentation. Your oral and written presentation must include the following tasks (minimum 100 words per answer, plus the necessary diagrams, graphs, and charts):

1. What options for a development strategy does Ocean Sound College have for developing a new system? Provide a brief explanation of specific alternatives that should be considered if development continues including in-house development and other strategies that would be a good fit. Justify your suggestions by analyzing the advantages and disadvantages of the chosen methods.
2. You have been asked to prepare a system requirements document and deliver a presentation to the housing office management. What should be the main elements of the system requirements document?
3. What financial analysis tools are available to calculate total cost of ownership for the system? What are the advantages (and possible disadvantages) of each tool?
4. Develop a cost-benefit analysis (include a spreadsheet, graph and/or diagram), using payback analysis, ROI, and present value (assume a discount rate of six percent).

Additional Information and Grading

The assignment is worth a total of 100 points and will be graded based on the following point allocation.

- 20 points for the Task 1 - Explanation of plan/strategies
- 20 points for the Task 2 - List and explanation of main elements of the system requirements
- 20 points for the Task 3 - List and explanation of available systems analysis tools
- 40 points for the Task 4 – Cost-benefit analysis

The Deliverables

Word Document and Excel Workbook
Submit copies of your Task 4 Cost-benefits Analysis spreadsheet/graph/diagram(s) as an Excel Workbook and your answers for Tasks 1 through 3 as a Word Document.

CASE 14 - NIPPON SUSHI & SASHIMI SHACK:
SYSTEM ARCHITECTURE

Introduction

Sushi Chefs Dianna Good and Charles Cerallo are partners in a west coast sushi restaurant, the Nippon Sushi and Sashimi Shack, they started six years ago. They are now interested in opening new locations and believe a computerized system will help with managing the restaurants after the expansion.

Background

You have been contracted to build the new information system for their current restaurant that currently uses a paper-based system. At this point, Nippon Sushi and Sashimi Shack has accepted your recommendation to install a server, switch, and five workstation computers as clients on a local area network. One of the workstations will be set up as a point of sales system. The network will include a backup unit, a high volume laser printer, and an impact printer for carbon copy forms that will be accessible by any one of the five workstations, and a Wi-Fi router.

SQL Ledger, an open source electronic accounting and business platform, will be used as the principal application for handling reservations, inventory records, sales, purchases and billing, barcode and label printing, invoice consolidation, a payroll module, and email and phone support. Now you will determine system architecture for the Nippon Sushi and Sashimi Shack.

Diagrams of Network Topologies

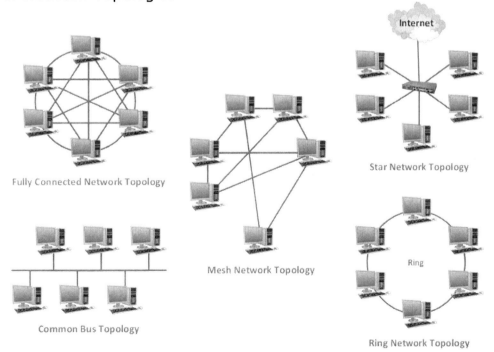

Figure 12 – General Network Topologies

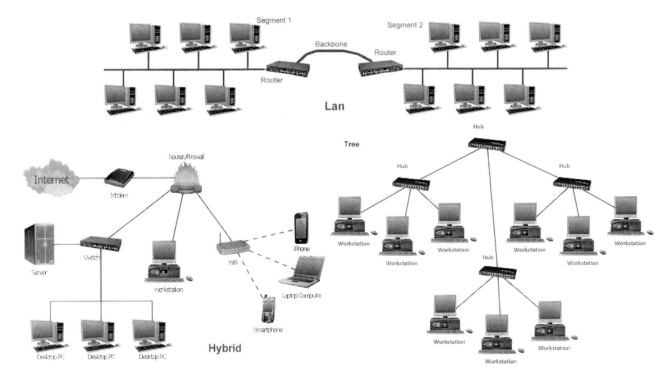

Figure 13 – General Network Topologies (cont.)

Your Task

1. What network model would be the best choice for the Nippon Sushi and Sashimi Shack? Compare and contrast three networking topographies discussing the advantages and disadvantages of each.
2. Using Lucidchart (https://www.lucidchart.com/) and the resources and components described above, diagram the network topography that you have chosen.
3. What would be the advantages of selecting an Internet-based architecture for the Nippon Sushi and Sashimi Shack system?
4. What would be the benefits of using a wireless network? What would be the drawbacks?
5. What would be the pros and cons of selecting in-house development versus a packaged solution for the Nippon Sushi and Sashimi Shack system?

Additional Information and Grading

The assignment is worth a total of 150 points and will be graded based on the following point allocation.

- 25 points for the Task 1 - Comparison and choice of a network model
- 50 points for the Task 2 - Network Diagram
- 25 points for the Task 3 - Advantages and Disadvantages of an Internet-based architecture
- 25 points for the Task 4 - Advantages and Disadvantages of a wireless network
- 25 points for the Task 5 - Advantages and Disadvantages of in-house and packaged solutions

The Deliverables

Word Document
Submit your diagram and information/answers in a Word Document.

CASE 15 - SUSHI HEIGHTS: SYSTEMS IMPLEMENTATION

Introduction

You are a systems analyst contracted-out by Sushi Heights Corporation to one of its subsidiaries, Cornucopia, an Internet-based retail company that sells earth friendly restaurant and dining products. You and your consulting firm have recently completed development of a new system for managing orders and inventory for Cornucopia. System architecture has already been decided, and you are ready to embark upon installation, evaluation, and training for the new system. Cornucopia was started seven years ago by its founder, Aidan Perry. It has grown from an in-home business to a company that employs five people in addition to the business owner, and has office and warehouse space in an office park designed to encourage small businesses. The business has relied upon a simple point of sales system that requires manual processes for taking orders, billing, and managing inventory. The new IS will provide the support necessary for the company to expand. None of the employees have worked with an IS system similar to the one designed.

Your Task

1. What types of testing should be performed? What types of test data should be used?
2. Develop a data conversion plan that specifies which data items must be entered, the order in which the data should be entered, and which data items are the most time-critical.
3. Discuss what options Cornucopia should consider for a changeover method for the new transaction system and provide specific reasons to support your choice.
4. The management of Cornucopia has decided to perform a post-implementation evaluation to assess the quality of the system. Who should be involved in the process? What investigative techniques should be used and why?

Additional Information and Grading

The assignment is worth a total of 100 points and will be graded based on the following point allocation.

- 25 points for the Task 1 - Data
- 50 points for the Task 2 - Conversion Plan
- 25 points for the Task 3 - Change Options
- 25 points for the Task 4 - Post-implementation Evaluation

The Deliverables

Word Document
Submit your diagram and information/answers in a Word Document.

CASE 16 - AMAZON.COM
(adopted and modified from
"Management Information Systems Cases"
by Gerald V. Post)

Introduction

In 1994, with a handful of programmers and a few thousand dollars in workstations and servers, Jeff Bezos set out to change the retail world when he created Amazon.com (ticker: AMZN). Shel Kaphan, Amazon's first programmer, assisted by others, including Paul Bar-ton-Davis, used a collection of tools to create Web pages based on a database of 1 million book titles compiled from the Library of Congress and Books in Print databases. Initially, Amazon was dependent on commercial and free database systems, as well as HTTP server software from commercial and free sources. Many of the programming tools were free software". In July 1995, Amazon opened its Web site for sales. Using heavily discounted book prices (20 to 30 percent below common retail prices); Amazon advertised heavily and became the leading celebrity of the Internet and e-commerce

Background

Amazon made its initial mark selling books, and many people still think of the company in terms of books. However, almost from the start, the company has worked to expand into additional areas—striving to become a global retailer of almost anything. Some of the main events include: 1995 books, 1998 music and DVD/video, 1999 auctions, electronics, toys, zShops/MarketPlace, home improvement, software, and video games (Brandt, 2011).

By the end of 1999, the company had forged partnerships with several other online stores, including Ashford.com, Audible, Della.com, drugstore.com, Gear.com, Green-light.com, HomeGrocer.com, Kozmo.com, living.com, NextCard.com, Pets.com, and Sotheby's. Of course, most of those firms and Web sites later died in the dot-com crash of 2000/2001.

Amazon also established partnerships with several large retailers, including Target, Toys 'R' Us, Babies 'R' Us, and Circuit City. Effectively, Amazon became a service organization to manage the online presence of these large retailers. However, it also uses its distribution system to deliver the products. The Circuit City arrangement was slightly different from the others—customers could pick up their items directly from their local stores (Heun, 2001). After Circuit City went under, the relationship ended.

By mid-2003, the Web sales and fulfillment services amounted to 20 percent of Amazon's sales. Bezos points out that most companies realize that only a small fraction of their total sales (5 to 10 percent) will come from online systems, so it makes sense to have Amazon run those portions.

In 2001, Amazon took over the Web site run by its bricks-and-mortar rival Borders. In 2000, Borders lost $18.4 million on total online sales of $27.4 million (Heun, 2001). Also in 2001, Amazon partnered with Expedia to offer travel services directly from the Amazon site. However, in this case, the Amazon portion consists of little more than an advertising link to the Expedia services. The deals in 2001 continued with a twist when Amazon licensed its search technology to AOL. AOL invested $100 million in Amazon and payed an undisclosed license fee to use the search-and-personalization service on Shop@AOL (Heun, 2001). In 2003, Amazon launched a subsidiary just to sell its Web-sales and fulfillment technology to other firms. Bezos noted that Amazon spends about $200 million a year on information technology (a total of

$900 million to mid-2003). The purpose of the subsidiary is to help recover some of those costs—although Bezos believes they were critically necessary expenditures.

With so many diverse products, and relationships, it might be tempting to keep everything separate. However, Amazon perceives advantages from showing the entire site to customers as a single, broad entity. Yes, customers click to the various stores to find individual items. But, run a search and you will quickly see that it identifies products from any division. Additionally, the company is experimenting with cross sales. In 2002, the Project Ruby test site began selling name-brand clothing and accessories. Customers who spent $50 or more on apparel received a $30 gift certificate for use anywhere else on Amazon.

By 2004, 25 percent of Amazon's sales were for its partners. But, one of Amazon's major relationships took a really bad turn in 2004 when Toys 'R' Us sued Amazon and Amazon countersued. The complaint by Toys 'R' Us alleges that it had signed a ten-year exclusivity contract with Amazon and had so far paid Amazon $200 million for the right to be the exclusive supplier of toys at Amazon.com. David Schwartz, senior VP and general counsel for Toys 'R' Us stated that "We don't intend to pay for exclusivity we're not getting" (Claburn, 2004). Amazon's initial response was that "We believe we can have multiple sellers in the toy category, increase selection, and offer products that (Toys 'R' Us) doesn't have" (Claburn, 2004). The lawsuit counters that at least one product (a Monopoly game) appears to be for sale by third-party suppliers as well as Toys 'R' Us. A month later, Amazon countersued, alleging that Toys 'R' Us experienced "chronic failure" to maintain sufficient stock to meet demand. The court documents noted that Toys 'R' Us had been out of stock on 20 percent of its most popular products (Claburn, June 2004). Although the dispute sounds damaging, it is conceivable that both parties are using the courts as a means to renegotiate the base contract.

Small merchants accelerated a shift to Amazon's marketplace technology. By 2007, Amazon was simply the largest marketplace on the Web. For example, John Wieber was selling $1 million a year in refurbished computers through eBay. But increased competition and eBay's rising prices convinced him to switch to direct sales through Amazon. Similar small merchants noted that although the fees on Amazon are hefty, they do not have to pay a listing fee. Plus, eBay shoppers only want to buy things at bargain-basement prices (Mangalindan, 2005).

In 2010, Target ended its contract with Amazon and launched its own Web servers. Amazon does not report sales separately for its partners such as Target, so it is difficult to determine what impact the change might have on Amazon. However, Amazon has many other sellers who offer similar products.

Digital Content

Amazon has been expanding its offerings in digital content—in many ways extending com-petition against Apple, but also leading the way in digital books. Although it was not the first manufacturer, Amazon is reportedly the largest seller of e-readers with the Kindle. Amazon does not report sales separately for the Kindle. Amazon also noted in 2011 that e-books for its Kindle reader have overtaken sales of paperback books as the most popular format. The e-books had already exceeded hard-cover books the year before (Wu, 2011). For many of these reasons, Borders, a bricks-and-mortar competitor to Amazon went under in 2011.

Amazon is also working to expand sales of music. The Web site has relatively standard pricing on current songs, but often offers discounts on older albums. By 2011, Amazon was also trying to expand into video streaming. Customers who pay $79 a year to join the Prime program gain faster shipping, and also access to a library of digital movies and TV shows. Unfortunately, with limited ties to the movie studios, the offerings initially were relatively thin. However, other video streaming sites, including Netflix and Hulu, were also struggling to develop long-term contracts with studios. In September 2011, Amazon announced a deal with Fox to offer movies and TV shows owned by the studio. At the same time, Netflix announced a similar deal with the Dreamworks studio. It will take time for studios to determine strategies on streaming video services and for consumers to make choices (Woo & Kung, 2011).

In late 2011, Amazon released its own version of a tablet computer. The company continued to sell the Kindle e-book reader, but the tablet focused on audio and video, using a color LCD display screen with a touch interface. Although it lacked features available on the market-leading Applet iPad, the Kindle table carried a price that was about half that of the iPad and other competitors ($200). The obvious goal was to provide a device that encourages customers to purchase more digital content directly from Amazon (Peers, 2011).

Sales Taxes

Sales taxes have been a long-term issue with Amazon. The Annual Report notes that sever-al states filed formal complaints with the company in March 2003. The basis for the individual suits is not detailed, but the basic legal position is that any company that has a physical presence in a state ("nexus" by the terms of a U.S. Supreme Court ruling), is subject to that state's laws and must then collect the required sales taxes and remit them to the state. The challenge is that the level of presence has never been clearly defined. Amazon argues that it has no physical presence in most states and is therefore not required to collect taxes. The most recent challenges are based on Amazon's "affiliate" program. Amazon pays a small commission to people who run Web sites and redirect traffic to the Amazon site. For instance, a site might mention a book and then include a link to the book on the Amazon site. Several states have passed laws claiming that these relationships constitute a "sales force" and open up Amazon to taxation within any state where these affiliates reside. In response, Amazon dropped the affiliate program in several states, has initiated a legal challenge in the state of New York, and in 2011, negotiated a new deal signed into law in California (Letzing, 2011). In the California deal, Amazon obtained a delay in collecting taxes for at least a year, in exchange for locating a new distribution center in the state and creating at least 10,000 full-time jobs. Amazon is also asking the U.S. Congress to create a new federal law to deal with the sales-tax issue. However, because the state sales tax issue is driven by the interstate commerce clause in the U.S. Constitution, a simple law will not alter the underlying principles. However, if Congress desired, it might create a Federal Sales tax law with some method of apportioning the money to states. But, do not bet on any major tax laws during a Presidential election year.

Information Technology

In the first years, Amazon intentionally kept its Web site systems separate from its order-fulfillment system. The separation was partly due to the fact that the programmers did not have the technical ability to connect them, and partly because the company wanted to improve security by keeping the order systems off the Web.

By 1997, Amazon's sales had reached $148 million for the year. The big book data-base was being run on Digital Alpha servers. Applications were still custom written in house. By early 2000, the company had over 100 separate database instances running on a variety of servers—handling terabytes of data.

In 2000, Amazon decided to overhaul its entire system. The company spent $200 million on new applications, including analysis software from Epiphany, logistics from Manugistics, and a new DBMS from Oracle. The company also signed deals with SAS for data mining and analysis (Collett, 2002). But, one of its biggest deals was with Excelon for business-to-business integration systems. The system enables suppliers to communicate in real time, even if they do not have sophisticated IT departments. It provides a direct connection to Amazon's ERP system either through programming connections or through a Web browser (Konicki, 2000).

About the same time (May, 2000), Amazon inked a deal with HP to supply new servers and IT services (Goodridge & Nelson, 2000). The new systems ran the open-source Linux operating system. Already by the third quarter of 2001, Amazon was able to reduce its IT costs by 24 percent from the same quarter in 2000 (Collett, 2002).

By 2004, the supply chain system at Amazon was a critical factor in its success. Jeffrey Wilke, Senior VP of worldwide operations, observed that "When we think about how we're going to grow our company, we focus on price, selection, and availability. All three de-pend critically on the supply chain" (Bacheldor, 2004).

Almost the entire system was built from scratch, customized to Amazon's needs. When a customer places an order, the system immediately connects to the distribution centers, determines the best way to ship the product, and provides the details to the customer in under two minutes. The entire process is automatic.

Dr. Russell Allgor moved from Bayer Chemical to Amazon and built an 800,000-equation computer model of the company's sprawling operation. When implemented, the goal of the model was to help accomplish almost everything from scheduling Christmas overtime to rerouting trucks in a snowstorm. Allgor's preliminary work focused on one of Amazon's most vexing problems: How to keep inventory at a minimum, while ensuring that when someone orders several products, they can be shipped in a single box, preferably from the warehouse — the company had six — that is nearest the customer (Hansell, 2001). Dr. Allgor's analysis is simple, but heretical to Amazon veterans. Amazon should increase its holdings of best sellers and stop holding slow-selling titles. It would still sell these titles but order them after the customer does. Lyn Blake, a vice president who previously ran Amazon's book department and now oversees company relations with manufacturers, disagrees with this perspective. "I worry about the customer's perspective if we suddenly have a lot of items that are not available for quick delivery."

Amazon's merchant and MarketPlace systems are powerful tools that enable smaller stores to sell their products through Amazon's system. Amazon continually works to improve the connections on those systems. This system caused problems in 2001—the main issue was that the data on the merchant Web sites was being updated only once every eight hours. The merchant's link to Amazon's main database servers, and internal applications transfer the data onto the displayed page as requested. As customers purchased items, the inventory quantities were altered in the main servers, but the current totals were not transferred to the display pages until several hours later. Consequently, customers would be told that an item was in stock, even it had sold out several hours ago. To solve the problem, Amazon installed Excelon's ObjectStore database in 2002. The system functions as a cache management server, reducing the update times from eight hours down to two minutes. Paul Kotas, engineering director for the Merchants@Group noted that "with the growth of this business, we needed a zero-latency solution" (Whiting, 2002).

In 2003, Amazon added a simple object access protocol (SOAP) gateway so that retailers could easily build automated connections to the system. Data is passed as XML documents and automatically converted to Amazon's format (Babcock, 2003).

One of the most successful technologies introduced by Amazon is the affinity list. When someone purchases an item, system makes recommendations based on similar items purchased by other customers. The system uses basic data mining and statistical tools to quickly run correlations and display the suggested products. Kaphan notes that "There was always a vision to make the service as useful as possible to each user and to take advantage of the ability of the computer to help analyze a lot of data to show people things they were most likely to be interested in" (Collett, 2002). The system also remembers every purchase made by a customer. So, the Amazon programmers created the Instant Order Update feature, that reminds customers if they have already purchased an item in their cart. Bezo notes that "Customers lead busy lives and cannot always remember if they've already purchased a particular item." He also observed that "When we launched Instant Order Update, we were able to measure with statistical significance that the feature slightly reduced sales. Good for customers? Definitely. Good for shareowners? Yes, in the long run" (2003 annual report).

Capital expenditures for software and Web site development are not cheap: $176 million, $146 million, and $128 million for 2010, 2009, and 2008 respectively (2010 Annual Report). But, in comparison, in 2010, net income tax provisions were $352 million.

New Services

Amazon requires huge data centers and high-speed Internet connections to run its systems. Through vast economies of scale, Amazon is able to achieve incredibly low prices for data storage and bandwidth. Around 2005, the company decided that it could leverage those low costs into a new business selling Internet-based services. The company offers an online data storage service called S3. For a monthly fee of about 15 cents per gigabyte stored plus 15 cents per gigabyte of data transferred, any person or company can transfer and store data on Amazon servers (Markoff, 2006). Through a similar service (EC2), any company can use the company's Web servers to deliver digital content to customers. The company essentially serves as a Web host, but instead of paying fixed costs, you pay 10 cents per virtual server per hour plus bandwidth costs. Amazon's network can handle bursts up to 1 gigabit per se-cond. The system creates virtual servers, running the Linux kernel, and you can run any software you want (Gralla, 2006). By 2011, the company had several locations providing S3 and EC2 Web services. It also offered online relational database services using either MySQL or the Oracle DBMS. Anyone can pay to store data in the DBMS, with charges being levied per hour, per data stored, and per data transferred. The point is that Amazon handles all of the maintenance and other companies avoid fixed costs. Even government agencies are adopting the benefits of storing data in these cloud services—including those run by Amazon. For example, the U.S. Treasury Department moved is public Web sites to the Amazon cloud. (Pratt, 2011).

Perhaps the most unusual service is Mturk. The name derives from an 18-century joke where a "mechanical" chess-playing machine surprised European leaders and royalty by beating many expert players. The trick was that a human was hidden under the board and moved the pieces with magnets. Amazon's trick is to use human power to solve problems. Companies post projects on the Mturk site and offer to pay a price for piecemeal work. Any individual can sign up and perform a task and get paid based on the amount of work completed. Amazon takes a 10 percent commission above the fee. For example, the company Casting Words places audio files on the site and pays people 42 cents to transcribe one minute of audio files into text (Markoff, 2006).

The Amazon EC2 and S3 services suffered some problems in the summer of 2011. A configuration error during an upgrade in the East Coast facility triggered a cascade that delayed all services in the facility. Internet services including Foursquare and Reddit that used the facility were impacted by the problems for almost a week (Tibken, 2011). Amazon engineers learned a lot from the problems and the same issue is unlikely to occur again (http://aws.amazon.com/message/65648/). But, the outage points out the risks involved in any centralized system. Ironically, the main problems were caused by algorithms designed to copy data to multiple servers to reduce risks. On the other hand, with multiple facilities, Amazon provides the ability to spread content and risk across multiple locations.

Adam Selipsky, vice president of product management and developer relations at Amazon Web Services observed that ""Amazon is fundamentally a technology company; we've spent more than one and a half billion dollars investing in technology and content. We began by retailing books, but it was never in our business plan to stay with that" (Gralla, 2006).

Financial Performance

When Amazon started, it spent huge amounts of money not only building infrastructure, but also buying market share. It took Amazon nine years to achieve profitability. And the profits started to arrive only after the company changed its pricing model—focusing on re-tail prices for popular items and smaller discounts for all books. In the process, the company lost almost $3 billion. It was not until 2009 that Amazon had generated enough profits to cover all of its prior losses (ignoring interest rates and debt).

The company's financial position has improved since 2000. Most of the improvement is due to increases in sales—which is good. But, those sales increased largely by selling products for other firms, and from one more twist. Amazon no longer discounts most of the books that it sells. In fact, it is generally more expensive to purchase books from Amazon than to buy them from your local bookstore. For competitive online pricing, check www.campusi.com, which searches multiple Web sites for the best price, but the selection might not be as large.

Year	Net Sales	Net Income	Debt (LT)	Equity	Employees
2010	34,204	1,152	1,561	6,864	33,700
2009	24,509	902	1,192	5,257	24,300
2008	19,166	645	896	2,672	20,700
2007	14,835	476	1,282	1,197	17,000
2006	10,711	190	1,247	431	13,900
2005	8,490	359	1,480	246	12,000
2004	6,921	588	1,835	(227)	9,000
2003	5,264	35	1,919	(1,036)	7,800
2002	3,933	(149)	2,277	(1,353)	7,500
2001	3,122	(567)	2,156	(1,440)	7,800
2000	2,762	(1,411)	2,127	(967)	9,000
1999	1,640	(720)	1,466	266	7,600
1998	610	(125)	348	139	2,100
1997	148	(31)	77	29	614
1996	16	(6)	0	3	
1995	0.5	(0.3)	0	3	

Table 5 - Financial Performance from Annual Reports ($Million)

The company's financial position has improved since 2000. Most of the improvement is due to increases in sales - which is good. But, those sales increased largely by selling products for other firms, and from one more twist. Amazon no longer discounts most of the books that it sells. In fact, it is generally more expensive to purchase books from Amazon than to buy them from your local bookstore. For competitive online pricing, check www.campusi.com, which searches multiple Web sites for the best price, but the selection might not be as large.

Another source of increased sales is the international market (largely Britain, Europe and Japan). Notice in the table that media sales (books, audio, and movies) are higher in the International market than in North America. More products are sold in North America, but clearly the growth path is the international market.

Net Sales 2010	North America	International
Media	$6,881	$8,007
Electronics + gen. merchandise.	10,998	7,365
Other	828	125

Table 6 - National & International Net Sales, 2010 ($Million)

Out of curiosity, where did all of that money go? In 2003, Bezos noted that $900 mil-lion went to business technology; $300 million was spent on the fulfillment centers; and $700 million on marketing and customer acquisition (Murphy, 2003). That last part largely represents selling books at a loss or offering free shipping while trying to attract customers. Those numbers add up to the $1.9 billion debt, but what happened to the other $1 billion in net losses? Interestingly, according to the 2010 Annual Report, Amazon still runs a loss on shipping. In 2010, the company declared shipping revenue of $1.2 billion, against outbound shipping costs of $2.6 billion, for a net loss of $1.4 billion! Amazon continues to expand aggressively. In 2011, Amazon estimated revenue in-creases of 28-39 percent but increased operating expenses by about 38 percent. Tom Szkutak, Amazon's finance chief noted that "When you add something to the magnitude of 23 fulfillment centers, mostly in the course of the second half of last year, you have added costs and you're not as productive on those assets for some time," (Wu, 2011).

For the longer term, Amazon's leaders clearly indicate that they are aware of the stiff competition—both from bricks-and-mortar retailers and from online rivals including small start-ups and established rivals including Apple and Google.

Your Task

Please answer the following questions using the information provided in the previous sections.

1. Who are Amazon's competitors?
2. Why would customers shop at Amazon if they can find better prices elsewhere?
3. Why did Amazon create most of its own technology from scratch?
4. If Amazon buys products from other firms and simply ships them to customers, why does it need so many of its own distribution centers?
5. Will other retailers buy or lease the Web software and services from Amazon? Can Amazon make enough money from selling these services?
6. Write a report to management that describes the primary cause of the problems, a detailed plan to solve them, and show how the plan solves the problems and describe any other benefits it will provide (1500 words minimum).

Additional Information and Grading

The assignment is worth a total of 150 points and will be graded based on the following point allocation.

- 20 points for the Tasks 1 through 5 - Case Study questions
- 100 points for the Task 6 - Report (1500 words minimum)

The Deliverables

Word Document
Submit your question answers and report in two separate Word Documents, APA standard format.

CASE 17 – WAL-MART.COM

(adopted and modified from
"Management Information Systems Cases"
by Gerald V. Post's)

Introduction

Wal-Mart is one of the largest companies in America. It is definitely the largest retailer, both in terms of the number of stores (8,970 worldwide in 2011) and the level of sales ($419 billion from the 2011 Annual Report). By pushing suppliers to continually reduce costs, Wal-Mart is known for pursuing low prices and the stores often attract customers solely interested in lower prices. With Wal-Mart's expansion into groceries, the company has be-come the largest retail grocer in America. Even by 2002, over 100 million Americans visit a Wal-Mart store in a given week (Press Action, 2002). Yet, Wal-Mart has struggled in the online world. The company has tried several approaches to selling physical and digital products online. From electronics to books, music, and movie rentals, the company has announced many different online stores. Wal-Mart has struggled with most of its attempts, while Amazon continues to grow and expand in e-commerce sales. Although Amazon has a fraction of the total sales of Wal-Mart, Amazon is substantially larger in online sales. Which raises the ultimate question of what Wal-Mart is doing wrong, or what it needs to do to get a larger share of online sales.

Background

Many articles and business cases have been written about Wal-Mart. Most customers are probably familiar with the store and the overall concepts, but a considerable amount of work takes place to manage the large inventory, suppliers, pricing, customers, and employees. Wal-Mart has been a leader in using information technology to reduce costs. A huge part of succeeding in retailing is to provide the right products in the stores at the right price, when customers want to buy them. To succeed, Wal-Mart needs to forecast demand for every product in every store. Each product can have multiple variations—such as size or color. Individual items are commonly identified with an SKU number (stock-keeping unit), pronounced "skew." Any Wal-Mart store has tens of thousands of SKUs. Of course, all of this data needs to be tracked by IT. Wal-Mart also can track personal purchases—based on credit and debit cards. All of the data from every store is collected and sent to the central servers at Bentonville, Arkansas.

In 2002, Wal-Mart primarily focused on using its home-grown custom code on its centralized systems (Lundberg, 2002). In an interview, CIO Kevin Turner noted that a key to Wal-Mart's success was continued striving to improve. His goals for the IT organization are to (1) run a centralized operation, (2) use common platforms, and (3) "be merchants first and technologists second." His first two conditions are important to holding down costs. It also makes it easier to transfer personnel among stores. Turner noted that the process was challenging when the standardized systems were first introduced to stores in other countries. The answer was to build a flexible system that still allowed local managers to make decentralized decisions but using centralized data. Turner emphasizes the importance of matching IT to the business needs—and simplifying all tasks. As one step in developing systems, the IT department requires developers to go out and perform the function before writing system specifications or designing changes. For example, a developer might spend a day working a cash register to understand the pressure and data-entry requirements.

Even as early as 2002, Wal-Mart was working on RFID. With an effort to reduce costs per chip, the ultimate goal was to replace bar codes with RFID chips. Even using the chips at the warehouse level would make it easier and faster to identify and route packages. Even in the store, finding products can be a problem. Carolyn Walton (no relation to the, founder), an analyst noted that when she was working on the floor, it once took them three days to find a box of a specific hair spray in the back room—resulting in lost sales. If the box had been tagged with RFID, it could have been found in minutes with a hand-held scanner.

Turner noted that Wal-Mart also spends a considerable amount of time in the re-search labs of its technology partners—working with universities and companies to see which technologies will be useful and how they might be modified to apply to Wal-Mart's problems.

In 2003, Linda Dillman became CIO of Wal-Mart (Sullivan, 2004). One of her biggest projects was the introduction of RFID tags, but the IT department was also working on 2,500 business-technology projects. As with most projects, the bulk of the RFID work was done using in-house programmers and software—with no outsourcing. Despite its large staff and heavy involvement, Wal-Mart spends less than typical retailers on IT—below one percent of worldwide revenue.

In 2004, a 423-terabyte Teeradata system was the heart of the system used to store and analyze the main sales data. Data is collected from the stores on an hourly basis, cleaned and transferred to the data warehouse. Managers can monitor sales in real time and make almost instant corrections on the sales floor. In terms of e-commerce, the company eventually moved to IBM's WebSphere system—largely for its scalability.

In 2006, Linda Dillman repeated the main points that drive the IT department: (1) merchants first, (2) common systems and platforms, and (3) centralized information systems. A secondary benefit of the centralized approach is that the data warehouse (RetailLink) is provided to the suppliers—who can also monitor sales in real time to help them plan production runs. The system also enables them to track the status of ships through the distribution centers to the retail stores. Providing another set of eyes and analysts in tracking sales and shipments.

By 2010, Wal-Mart was processing over one million customer transactions an hour; generating databases estimated to contain at least 2.5 petabytes (Economist, 2010). Rollin Ford, the CIO in 2010 emphasized the importance of processing and analyzing the huge amount of data: "Every day I wake up and ask 'how can I flow data better, manager data better, analyze data better,'" (Economist, 2010).

E-Commerce

In 2011, Wal-Mart appears to have shifted part of its online strategy. Two leading managers, Raul Vazquez in charge of global e-commerce in developed markets, and Steve Nave, who ran the California-based Wal-Mart.com left the company (Bustillo, 2011). The company also announced that it was ending the sale of downloaded music (a step they had also taken years before). Part of the restructuring appears to shift e-commerce responsibility to man-agers in individual nations. Regional managers were appointed to be in charge of nations within specific sectors, such as Latin America, Asia, and Europe.

Although Wal-Mart does not report sales for the e-commerce division, Internet Retailer estimates that in the U.S. and Canada, Wal-Mart generates about $4 billion in sales—making it the sixth largest—behind not only Amazon, but Staples and Office Depot (Bustillo, 2011). Interestingly, Wal-Mart, through ASDA provides online grocery shopping in Britain.

Vudu

Wal-Mart bought Vudu in 2010 for a reported $100 million; an online site that provides rentals and purchases of digital downloads for Hollywood movies. Within a year, the site had become the third-most popular streaming site on the Web. However, the big two (iTunes at 65.8 percent and Microsoft Zune Video at 16.2 percent) dominate the 5.3 percent market share of Vudu. On the other hand, Wal-Mart dropped its music downloads in 2011 because of poor performance. Edward Lichty, Vudu General Manager, noted that "offering first-run movies a la carte is doing very well right now and has tripled so far this year," (Bustillo & Talley, 2011). Tablet owners (including the iPad) can download movies through a browser interface, which means Vudu does not have to pay Apple's 30 percent commission fee. Vudu also has agreements in place with most major studios, including the rights to stream and sell high-definition movies. However, it is not clear how Vudu connects to Wal-Mart sales, or that customers even know Vudu is owned by Wal-Mart.

Amazon and Sales Taxes

Under pressure from local retailers—presumably including Wal-Mart—state governments are trying to enact laws that directly affect Amazon. In particular, Amazon has long avoided collecting state sales taxes on sales by arguing that the company does not have a physical presence in most states. However, in an attempt to attract more sales to its site, several years ago Amazon established an "affiliate" program where anyone with a Web site could set up a link to direct potential customers to Amazon. The partners then collected a tiny percentage of the sales revenue. Several states rewrote their tax laws to define these "partnerships" as creation of a physical "nexus" that opened the door to taxing all sales from Amazon. In response, Amazon dropped the program in several states, challenged the law directly in New York, and then offered a compromise in California (The Wall Street Journal 9/11/2011). The compromise, signed in September 2011, delays the collection of taxes from Amazon for one year and allows Amazon to run its affiliate program in California. At one point, Amazon suggested that it would also build a new distribution center to bring jobs to California, but it is not clear if that provision survived the negotiations. Overall, retail stores and legislatures are trying to "level the playing field" so that all purchases will be subject to state sales taxes. Technically, the state laws are written so that citizens of a state who purchase items from out-of-state vendors are required to pay the "use taxes" even when the seller does not collect them. The state tax forms have an entry line for listing the purchases and the tax owed. Only a few people voluntarily pay this tax. States continue to stretch the definitions to force out-of-state companies to collect the taxes, but they have lost every court case at the U.S. Supreme Court because the U.S. Constitution forbids states from interfering with interstate commerce.

Amazon and Target

For several years, Target, a direct competitor to Wal-Mart, relied on Amazon to handle its Web sales. The Amazon Web site displayed the products and processed the payments. In most cases, Amazon also handled the warehouse operations, shipped the products, and handled customer service. Essentially, Target outsourced the entire Web operations to Amazon. After two-years in development, in 2011, Target launched its own Web site. At that point, Target will stop selling items on Amazon's site. In 2010, Target had $1.33 billion in U.S. sales, making it the 23rd largest online retailer. (Zimmerman & Talley, 2011). Target

said the new Web site will more closely match the in-store experience and that it will be able to carry a bigger assortment of products—with as many as 800,000 products with free shipping (probably free to pick up at a local store).

Wal-Mart Sales Data

In 2011, Wal-Mart shook up the marketing world by declaring that sales data from its stores was a strategic asset and the company would no longer provide access to the data to outsiders. A decade later, in July 2011, Wal-Mart agreed to provide access to its sales data to Nielsen—the market research company. In the meantime, the sales climate had changed, from the high-increases of the early 2000s to eight-consecutive quarters of declining sales in 2010 from stores open at least a year. Cindy Davis, newly appointed as Wal-Mart executive vice president for global customer insights noted that "We plan to share our point-of-sale information to help us identify category growth opportunities sooner and collaborate with our manufacturer partners to develop more impactful customer-driven programs going for-ward" (Zimmerman & Lamar, 2011).

Your Task

Please answer the following questions using the information provided in the previous sections.

1. How is Wal-Mart's Web site different from Amazon and Office Depot?
2. Do Wal-Mart and Best Buy face the same problems or different ones?
3. What customers shop at Wal-Mart, both in-store and online?
4. Determine a strategy for Wal-Mart to improve online sales.
5. How difficult will it be for Wal-Mart's competitors to build similar features in their Web sites? How long can Wal-Mart maintain its advantage?
6. Write a report to management that describes the primary cause of the problems, a detailed plan to solve them, and show how the plan solves the problems and describe any other benefits it will provide.

Additional Information and Grading

The assignment is worth a total of 150 points and will be graded based on the following point allocation.

- 20 points for the Tasks 1 through 5 - Case Study questions
- 100 points for the Task 6 - Report (1500 words minimum)

The Deliverables

Word Document
Submit your question answers and report in two separate Word Documents, APA standard format.

CASE 18 – NINTENDO
(adopted and modified from
"Management Information Systems Cases"
by Gerald V. Post's)

Introduction

The video game market has progressed through several stages in terms of hardware and software. But it has also faced many changes in leadership. The early battles were between Nintendo and Sega, but personal computers always had a role. Microsoft pushed this role by introducing its own game box. Then consumer-electronics giant Sony jumped into the battle and captured a big chunk of the market. The battles between manufacturers some-times depend on hardware and the ability of one manufacturer to leapfrog the others with an earlier introduction of the technology. Other times it comes down to creativity in games or other features.

In 1991, Sega was the first to introduce the Genesis game machine that used 16-bit computations for faster games and more detailed video displays. It was introduced in time for the 1991 Christmas season with several game cartridges available. Genesis also maintained compatibility with older games. With the technological lead on Nintendo, it looked as if Sega was ready to take the lead in the $6 billion dollar market for home video games. By Christmas, when Nintendo introduced its own Super NES 16-bit game, Sega held the lead in sales. Sega's gain came partly from introducing the machine earlier and partly by selling it for $50 less than Nintendo's machine. It also had more games available.

By most management measures, Sega Enterprises was ready for the huge Christmas season that began in September 1991. Its inventory system was automated, using Computer Associates' software on an IBM AS/400. Executives had personal computers loaded with Microsoft's Excel spreadsheet. Each night an EDI service bureau collected sales data over phone lines from 12,500 retail stores across the United States and passed them on to the Sega AS/400. Overnight, the computer created reports detailing sales of the Genesis ma-chines and corresponding game cartridges that were sold the day before. Additional reports could be created by the MIS department but often took days to create.

By any measure at that time, Sega Enterprises had all of the information managers needed. Yet, Sega of America executives were facing a crisis in 1991. They did not have sufficient access to the data to make correct decisions. The retail stores were furious because Sega could not deliver machines to them fast enough. To salvage this crucial selling time, Sega used air freight to ship the games directly from Japanese factories to the U.S. stores. Despite helping Sega to its best year (selling 1.6 million units), this emergency airlift was estimated to have increased Sega's costs by $10 million. To that number, according to one estimate, you can add in $75 million in sales lost to Nintendo, because customers switched to Nintendo when the Genesis machines were unavailable. Sega executives knew the cause of the problem: the corporation's internal information system did not provide sufficient access to the data. By the time managers received the daily sales reports, it was too late. Similarly, although executives could use spreadsheets to analyze the data to spot trends, the numbers all had to be rekeyed from the reports into the spreadsheets (Hutheesing, 1993; Computer Letter, 1993; and Halper, 1993).

Background

Nintendo was formed in 1889 to sell playing cards. Since 1949, it has been run by Hiroshi Yamauchi, who inherited the company from his grandfather. He made several at-tempts at diversification, but most of them failed. He found success by concentrating on toys and arcade games. The huge success of the 1980 Game & Watch provided money to in-vest in the video game market. The original game machine was sold at a low price (about $65), with the intention of making money later on the game cartridges. Introduced into the United States in 1985, it sold 440,000 the first year.

Nintendo strictly controls the production of games for its machines. In Japan, no other company can create games for the machine. The Federal Trade Commission disallowed that strict position in the United States. But even so, vendors must first get approval from Nintendo and pay a royalty fee for every cartridge sold—reportedly as much as $10 per cartridge for the early systems. After eight years of selling the original machine, Nintendo took a risk with the Super NES in 1990 by producing a machine that was incompatible with the earlier cartridges. Yet, in the 1990s, Sega was the dominant company in the video games market. (Halper, 1993; and, Calrton, 1995).

Before Christmas sales in 1993, Sega of America controlled almost 50 percent of the video game market, compared to the 7 percent it had in 1990. Sales in the U.S. division reached $1 billion. According to The Wall Street Journal (June 7, 1994, p. B2), the U.S. market for video game software was growing at the rate of 30 percent a year, and would total about $4.5 billion in 1994. Sega was actively developing interactive games based on CD-ROM technology. Nintendo had announced plans to introduce a CD-ROM component, but has repeatedly delayed production.

By 1994, Sega had still not resolved all of its delivery problems. For Christmas, the company released the Sega 32X game system as an upgrade to existing systems. It provided better graphics and sound, as well as faster action. Once again, Sega beat most of its rivals to the market and demand was high. The only catch was that owners of older Sega systems needed a special cable adapter to connect the game to older televisions that did not have separate audio and video inputs. Although the 32X machines were available, the $20 cables were impossible to find. Twelve-year-old Casey Overstreet pointedly observed that "You got this great game-playing system and you're going, 'All right!' Then you find out you can't play it" (Manning, 1994). Some retailers were not aware that the cable was needed, and Sega of America simply noted that it was sold out during the holiday season.

The Nintendo Approach

Nintendo took a slightly different approach to the distribution issue. In 1989, Nintendo had 130 merchandising representatives who traveled to retail outlets. At each store, they recorded 14 pieces of data such as sales floor inventories, prices, and allocated shelf space. The data was recorded on forms that were mailed to headquarters and entered into the central computer. It often took one to two months for the data to be compiled into a report. Mark Thorien of Nintendo noted that "By that time, the information was so untimely that it was basically worthless . . . There are real dramatic swings between what people want one day and what they want the next. You have to stay on top of it, or you get stuck with a lot of inventory that you can't sell" (Halper, 1993).

In 1989, Nintendo replaced the paper-based system with hand-held computers for all of the sales representatives. As data was entered into the machine, it was automatically transmitted back to the central computer. Messages could also be sent to from the corporate managers down to the sales representatives. Reports were now created in 24 hours. Additionally, there were fewer mistakes because of misread handwriting.

In November 1993, Nintendo of America signed a contract with Unisys to provide "Fast EDI" services between Nintendo and 15,000 retail stores. With the old methods, it took an average of five weeks for a licensee of a Nintendo cartridge to ship products to the stores. The new method was supposed to cut the time down to six days. The system gained speed by allowing licensees to store their products at the Nintendo central warehouse in North Bend, Washington. The EDI ordering system tied to the stores was capable of processing sales for 15 million cartridges a year. By centralizing the warehouse and the EDI system, Nintendo could provide faster delivery of cartridges at a lower cost than licensees could obtain on their own. At the end of 1993, 11 retail chains had signed up for the system. Almost two-thirds of Nintendo games were produced by licensees. Most were small companies. Phil Rogers, vice president of operations at Nintendo, estimates that a comparable system would cost the licensees between $20,000 and $500,000 each, which the smaller companies could not afford. With the new system, a per-cartridge fee is paid to Nintendo and a separate fee to Unisys.

1995 and 32-bits

By 1993, Nintendo's U.S. market share in 16-bit games had slipped to 39 percent. In February 1994 Hiroshi Yamauchi, head of the Japanese parent company, removed his son-in-law Minuro Arakawa as head of the U.S. subsidiary. He was replaced by Howard Lincoln who was chosen to be more aggressive. By 1995, with improved marketing and new games, Nintendo's market share had risen to 57 percent

However, 1995 and 1996 offered new challenges to Nintendo and Sega: the introduction of 64-bit game players capable of three-dimensional graphics. Sega and new rivals like 3DO were to have 64-bit systems ready for the 1995 Christmas season. Nintendo would not. A lack of 64-bit games held the market down for a year. The big question was whether Sega could use the six-month lead to gain a major advantage. Both Nintendo and Sega suffered in Christmas 1994 sales, with retail sales down approximately 20 percent. In October 1995, Microsoft announced a set of programming tools that would enable personal computers to function as better games machines. Microsoft's stated goal was to make the personal computer the premier video game platform.

In 1998, Nintendo introduced the Game Boy Color, selling 100 million units by 2000. The portable unit was a hit with consumers, and kids carried it everywhere (Nintendo history).

Microsoft and Sony

In November 2001, Microsoft launched the Xbox game platform. The system had a dedicated graphics card to handle high-speed 3D images, and a high-speed processor to provide realistic action, particularly in sports games. It was also the first video game system designed to play online broadband games, all for $300 (Microsoft press release January 8, 2002). Nintendo launched the competing Game Cube in September in Japan and November in the United States and became a top-selling game system (Nintendo history). Sony's PlayStation 2 had launched a year earlier and quickly gained market share. Although Sega's Dreamcast system was launched before the Sony PS2, Sony quickly trounced the Dreamcast. Sony over-hyped the system and was unable to meet the high demand when it was launched (Da-ta Monitor, 2004). However, the year lead helped overcome the initial production delays.

System	2004 Sales	Installed Base
Sony PlayStation 2	6.4	22.3
Microsoft Xbox	3.2	7.8
Nintendo Game Cube	3.3	6.8
Nintendo Game Boy Adv.	8.1	19.8

Table 7 – In millions of units, Gaudiosi 2004

The Sony PlayStation 2 quickly gained sales and became the leading game platform. Annual sales are only one indication of importance. To game developers, the installed base is critical because it defines the potential size of the market for the software. Sony PlayStation 2 held that lead for several years.

2006 Xbox 360 vs. PS3 vs. Wii

The 2006 holiday season was shaping up to become another battleground. The major hype was Microsoft's Xbox 360 versus Sony's PlayStation 3. Both were designed with major technical advances and targeted hard-core gamers. Both could produce high-definition TV out-put for the next generation of realism. The Xbox 360 had an option to include a Toshiba HD DVD player. Sony had a version with a Blu-Ray player. But, Microsoft launched first and gained mindshare and market share by launching almost a full year before the other manufacturers. Sony was the market leader in 2006 with100 million PlayStation 2 machines sold, and Microsoft was basically buying market share—losing billions of dollars on the original Xbox hardware. However, Sony struggled with delays in production of the PS3—particularly the Blu-Ray player. Sony managed to deliver only 197,000 systems to the U.S. market in 2006. In the end, it never really mattered. Some people expected long lines for the few PS3 systems that made it to the market, but the rush never materialized, partly because of the high price, but mostly because the Xbox was already out and everyone wanted the Nintendo Wii (Guth, 2006).

The hot seller for 2006 and 2007 was the Nintendo Wii. The Wii was radically different from the earlier Nintendo systems and the Xbox 360 and PS3. (1) The system was considerably less expensive ($250). (2) The games were straightforward and easy to learn. (3) The games used a radically new controller based on accelerometers that enabled users to control action by moving their arms and bodies, much as you would in a real sport. The launch of the Wii sold out 476,000 units in the U.S. which almost topped the Xbox 360 500,000 sales in November (Bettenhausen, 2007). Satoru Iwata, Nintendo president said that the company deliberately set out to expand the game market to consumers who rarely play videogames.

In mid-2007, Nintendo was cranking out over a million units a month—and still not meeting demand. Entirely new groups of customers were clamoring for the active games based on the controller designed by Shigeru Miyamoto. When they could get them, even elderly groups bought them—for bowling tournaments and other sporting contests. From Nintendo's perspective the news was great. Nintendo makes about $50 on every unit. Sony and Microsoft, relying on expensive state-of-the art technology, lose money on every ma-chine sold—hoping to make a profit on the games (O'Brien, 2007).

Nintendo is also efficient, with Iwata pushing cost cutting and pushing suppliers to provide better deals. With only 3,400 employees, Nintendo generated $8.26 billion in revenue in 2006 or $2.5 million per employee. Profits amounted to $1.5 billion or $442,000 per employee. In contrast, Microsoft generated $177,000 and Google, highly praised for its profitability, managed $288,000. When Iwata joined Nintendo, Sony's PS2 was king and Microsoft was battling Sony to see who could add the most advanced features to appeal to the hardcore gamers. Mr. Iwata said that "we decided that Nintendo was going to take another route—game expansion. We are not competing against Sony or Microsoft. We are battling the indifference of people who have no interest in videogames." The strategy is known as "blue ocean" based on a book by W. Chan Kim and Renee Mauborgne. Most industries have an intense rivalry in the primary market or "red ocean" (for the bloody fights). By moving into the open blue ocean, Nintendo leads the way into a new market with minimal competition at the start (O'Brien, 2007).

By July 2007, demand for the Wii was still outstripping supply. Part of the shortage was likely due to Nintendo managing the supply chain—it is difficult to ramp up to millions of units in one month and then falling back to zero the next. It is more efficient to maintain a steady production rate. But demand was still a huge factor. By July, 2.8 million Wii con-soles were sold in the United States, more than double the number of PS3 systems sold (CNN Online July 2, 2007). Some experts and Mr. Iwata began suggesting that the Wii could overtake the lifetime sales record of the PS2 of more than 100 million units. Sony cut the price of its PS3 by $100 in July, but experts did not expect the action to affect sales of the Wii (CNN Online July 13, 2007).

In July 2007, Microsoft realized that there was a hardware problem with the Xbox 360. The company had shipped more than 10 million consoles worldwide since November 2005, but several of them were crashing. Microsoft decided to support customers by extending the warranty to cover machines that were failing. The company took a $1 billion charge to cover the costs of the anticipated repairs (The Wall Street Journal,

2007).

Games Market 2011

Somewhat surprisingly, the three leading vendors in games machines (Sony, Nintendo, and Microsoft) made few changes to their underlying systems through 2011. The one notable exception was Microsoft's introduction of the Kinect controller. The Kinect uses dual video cameras to pick up three-dimensional movement by the user and feed this movement in-formation to the game. To a large degree, the Kinect went after the Wii market—completely removing the need for hand-held controllers. The Kinect was good for sports and activity-based games, but the lack of fine-motor control made it difficult for more complex games. Still, the revolutionary controller gained mindshare for Microsoft and put pressure on Nintendo. Possibly to counter this introduction, but also due to an industry-wide slump in sales, Sony cut the price of the PS 3 by $100 in August 1009 (Gallagher, 2009). The down-turn also affected Nintendo, which estimated sales of 20 million units for fiscal year 2010. By tapping new markets, the Wii had achieved the status as the market leader, with sales of more than 53 million units from its debut in 2006 to October 2009, compared to Sony with 24 million PS 3s and Microsoft with 34 million Xbox 360 units (Wakabayashi, 2009).

In 2010, Nintendo of America hired Ingvar Petursson as the new senior vice-president of information services. Jim Cannataro, executive VP of Administration noted that "He will be tasked with the multi-year project of modernizing our systems" (Harris, 2011).

Video

One new feature for games machines introduced in 2010 was the ability for game boxes to stream video to play movies. In Spring 2010, Nintendo announced a partnership with Netflix to stream rented videos through its game consoles. The Sony PS3 and Microsoft Xbox 370 already offered the Netflix service as well as access to their own online library of movies (Stynes, 2010).

Network Attacks

The primary games machines communicate across the Internet, but they essentially create their own networks to transfer specialized games data. The networks are also used for communication, purchasing games, and downloading games and updates. In 2011, the Sony network was attacked—apparently by criminals attempting to obtain credit card and other financial information. To stop the attack and fix the problem, Sony had to shut down its network for several weeks to rewrite the software. The discovery of the attack arrived at a critical time—when the Warner Brothers Mortal Kombat was released (Sherr, 2011). A couple of months later, Nintendo and Sega both announced that their networks had been at-tacked as well. Sega said the intruder stole personal information on almost 1.3 million users, but that financial data was not lost because Sega used an external provider to handle the payments (Wakabayashi, 2011).

The Nintendo network was also attacked, but the company noted that no personal data had been stolen. A collection of attackers calling themselves LulzSec claimed responsibility and posted a configuration file on its site as evidence. The LutlSec Web site chided Nintendo to fix the server configuration error saying "We like the N64 console too much—we sincerely hope Nintendo plugs the gap" (Stevenson, 2011). On the other hand, someone in Spain allegedly stole personal data on thousands of Nintendo users and attempted to blackmail the company. The man was arrested in February 2011 (Chawla, 2011).

Portable Devices

For a while, Nintendo controlled a market segment with its portable devices. Although the games were relatively simple, the portability factor and relatively low price of the device made it popular. Newer versions incorporated additional features and better screens, including the 3DS introduced in March 2011 which supported three-dimensional images without the use of special glasses (Web site history).

On the other hand, the Apple iPod, most cell phones, and tablets—particularly the market leading iPad—quickly became major rivals in the games market. Several reports pointed out that 80 percent of the applications on iTunes consist of games and entertainment. For young children, it might make sense to purchase standalone portable games. For anyone else (tens of million in the U.S. alone), it makes more sense to use a cell phone. Yet, Nintendo is pushing its handheld platform and refuses to create or release games for the iPhone (Evans, 2011). Although the 3DS was introduced in March, by August, Nintendo was forced to cut the price in Japan from ¥25,000 to ¥15,000. Similar cuts were planned in other markets (Williams 2011).

For the moment, cell phones lack the processing and graphics power to compete directly with the PS3 and Xbox. But with built-in accelerometers and touch screens, several types of games became popular. Squeezed in the portable market by cell phones, and lacking a major console platform, Nintendo would appear to be struggling to find new sales. But in September 2011, Nintendo was advertising for a contract programmer to design system stress tests for its "next gen console platform," so the company appears to be working on new systems (Job ad on Taleo.net).

Your Task

Please answer the following questions using the information provided in the previous sections.

1. Who are Nintendo's competitors?
2. Is Nintendo's strategy of leaving excess demand a good idea?
3. How can Nintendo know how many game systems to produce for the holiday season?
4. Nintendo has long had a policy of creating its own games. Is this idea good or bad?
5. How difficult will it be for Nintendo's competitors to build similar features in their products? How long can Nintendo maintain its advantage?
6. Write a report to management that describes the primary cause of the problems, a detailed plan to solve them, and show how the plan solves the problems and describe any other benefits it will provide.

Additional Information and Grading

The assignment is worth a total of 150 points and will be graded based on the following point allocation.

- 20 points for the Tasks 1 through 5 - Case Study questions
- 100 points for the Task 6 - Report (1500 words minimum)

The Deliverables

Word Document
Submit your question answers and report in two separate Word Documents, APA standard format.

APPENDIX A - STRATEGIC PLANNING EXAMPLES AND WORKSHEETS

Example 1

Description of Organization

Heartland PCA is a home health care organization based in Duluth Minnesota, with branch offices in Bemidji, Finlayson, and Hibbing. Up until this year we have kept paper records of all our clients and haven't kept any electronic records. Currently there isn't a specific IT department, but rather employees will call outside tech support for any issues they run into with the minimal computer bookkeeping they currently do. Our company is relatively small for a Home Health Care Organization. We organize the care of around 300 clients between our main office and three branch offices.

Heartland's Vision for the IT Department

We hope to establish an internal IT department at the Duluth office as we move towards electronic billing. The hope is that the IT department can be staffed with current employees as they are freed from many of the tasks that were involved with a paper filing system. Our hope is to make this transition as smooth as possible with as little interruption in billing as possible.

Goals for Heartland's IT Department
Research New Billing Software for PMAP Billing

The current program we use to bill for our Prepaid Medical Assistance Program clients is outdated and frequently does not save information properly. We would like to find another billing software that will support our billing needs. We would like to have this new software implemented by March of 2016. Our Duluth Branch Manager will be in charge of researching different options and then interviewing someone from the software company to find out what kinds of support they can provide for us.

Purchase New Computers for the Billing Department

Some of the computers in our billing department are out of date. We would like to purchase some new desktop PCs for the Duluth office, which is where all the billing is done for the PCA and Homemaking services we provide. We would like to have these computers in place before we implement the new billing software. Debbie Donald, our office manager, is in charge of researching prices, and looking to see if we can get a bulk discount. Debbie has been instructed to make sure the new computers are installed January 31, 2016.

Update the Operating System and Microsoft Office Suite On All Computers

To maintain as much uniformity across computers as possible, we would like all of the main office's computers to be updated to Windows 10 by February 29, 2016. Along with this update we will be purchasing a new subscription to the Microsoft Office Suite and will be moving away from using Office

2003. All current documents should, at the time of installation of the new software, be updated and used in the new Office 2016 software. While each person will be in charge of downloading and updating their own computers, Jarod Champeaux will be in charge of purchasing the new Microsoft Office subscription. Windows 10 is a free update since all of the computers are using, at a minimum, the Windows 7 OS. Anna Carlson will be put in charge of making sure everyone's computers have been updated.

Train Employees On How to Use New Billing Software

Once we select a billing software we will need to teach the employees how to use the new software. Our intention is to try to find a software company that will also provide training for their software. We plan to train our Billing Manager Anna Carlson and she will then be in charge of training her billing staff. This will all need to happen before she goes on maternity leave April 15, 2016.

Import Paper Based Data into New Billing System

Once our new billing system is in place we will need to transpose our paper based data and import it into the new software. This project will be accomplished between the dates of May 16, 2016 and September 6, 2016 while our billing clerk, Rachel Aiken, is on summer break. During this time, she will be working full time hours. Her duties will include scanning in service agreements, creating Excel documents that contain the old billing data that will be imported into the new software, and making sure old paper documents are disposed of in accordance with HIPAA standards.

Research and Purchase New Internet Security Software

Our current computers do not have any internet security software. We need to purchase software for all of our office computers in order to protect client data. Debbie Donald will be in charge of researching and finding a software that is licensed for an entire small business so we do not need individual licenses for each computer. This must be implemented before we start with our new billing software. Ideally it will be finished by January 31, 2016, but Debbie has been given until February 29, 2016 to finish this task.

Look into a Cloud Based Server to Link the Branch Offices to the Main Office

Currently our servers are decentralized and each branch office runs on its own server. We would like to make it so all the offices have access to a centralized set of documents. This will cut down on the amount of time employees spend calling the other branch offices. Deb Flynn will be put in charge of researching different private cloud based servers we can rent space from. We would like to have this put in place by September 1, 2016.

Example 2

Strategic Plan

(Lululemon is a clothing store/ brand that produces recreational outerwear to consumers of all ages. The organizational structure of the IT Department is decentralized and relies on a team environment.)

<u>**Store's Mission**</u>: All lululemon locations have strong ties to the local communities, allowing lululemon employees to get the community together for yoga sessions for all ages. Therefore they are creating components for people to live longer, healthier, and fun lives.

<u>**Stores' Vision**</u>: Lululemon will be widely regarded as a prestigious clothing line that promotes comfort and quality to customers of all ages. Not only do they want their customers to feel comfortable and confident, but they also want them to long healthy lives.

<u>**Information Technologies Vision**</u>: Information Technologies fosters an environment that promotes and enhances Lululemon's vision and exemplifies its mission to provide technologies that are of a high quality and easily accessible for all ages. This vision will be used to better the experience for staff and customers.

Goals for the upcoming year

A. To make it more convenient and beneficial for customers to exchange clothing that is damaged or not the appropriate size.
   a. With the creation of an app for Lululemon it will allow customers to send clothing, via image, if the clothing that they received is torn, wrong size, or not the quality that was expected. With this app, it would create a software that allows you to take pictures of the clothing you would like to exchange. The store would then receive these images and make a decision, determining whether or not they would be able to repair the damages or send you a replacement of the article of clothing.
   b. Target Completion Date: Fall 2016
   c. Jacque & Chrisi: It is their mission to design an app that honors the stores mission as well as serving their customers' needs.
   d. Components from text: Creation of a software- app, Reporting- Sending in feedback to the store, Privacy- ensuring pictures sent in are protected.

B. Development of a system that enables customers to easily see what sizes are available in store making it a more comfortable shopping experience.
   a. With the development of this system it allows customers to walk into the store and go to the computer to see what is directly available in the store in their size, so that they don't have to be searching franticly for their size, or a certain make that they may be looking for. Also showing where in the store the item of choice is located. Overall this would help the customers have a great experience while shopping. There are a lot of customers that don't have a local store near, so when those who live far away we want them to have a great experience, by using this software and web.
   b. *Target Completion Date*: January 2017
   c. *Jacque & Chrisi*: It is their responsibility to make a web page that shows the clothing in a database that can determine what is available in store for purchase.
   d. *Component from text*: Creation of software/ database- customers can access to see if size and clothing is in store.

C. Appeal to customers of all ages through images on the Lululemon website.
   a. With the ability to see the products on models of different ages and body types consumers will be more confident when purchasing an item. This can be accomplished by allowing you to enter your age or body type into the website and the images you see will honor what you have entered. This would require the creation of an updated website.
   b. *Target Completion Date*: February 2018
   c. *Jacque & Chrisi*: It is their responsibility to create a function that allows customers to change the model that they are seeing the clothing appear on. They need to update the website so that this function will be possible.
   d. *Component from text: Internet/Web* - using the online store website to see the different images.

D. Making it optional for consumers to customize clothing to their liking.
   a. With developing this type of system will allow for customers to personalize their own tops, sports bras, pants, boxers, etc. When customers come into the store there will be computers set up allowing customers to personalize a certain piece of clothing that they wish to customize. There can choose between different styles and colors.
   b. *Target Completion Date*: January 2017
   c. *Jacque & Chrisi*: It is their responsibility to meet customers' needs and help them design their personal clothing.
   d. *Components from text*: Internet/web- using function on website to design personal clothing, Privacy- keeping designs private and personal unless you want them to be shared.

Example 3

Organization and Description

The IT Department and Coding at Essentia Health. Essentia Health is headquartered in Duluth, Minnesota and they are an intergraded health system serving patients in a total of four states: Minnesota, Wisconsin, North Dakota, and Idaho.

Organizational Structure

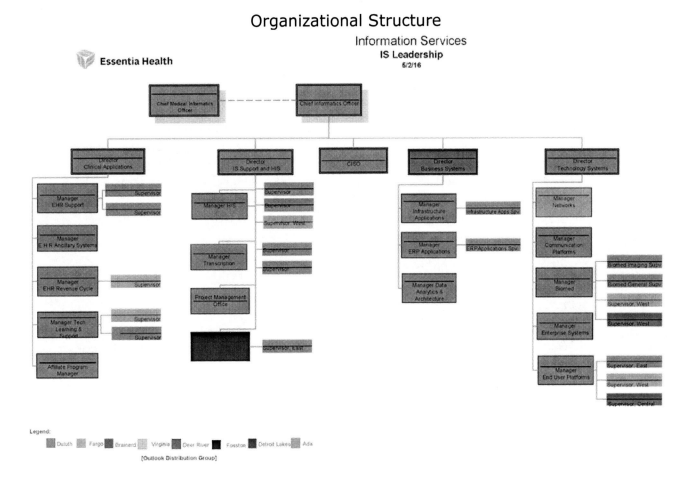

Organization Mission and Vision

"Our Mission, Vision, and Values provide a strong foundation for the work we do in order to make a healthy difference in people's lives. A framework that expresses our priorities in what we will achieve and how we will achieve them."

Goals and Action Plan

Since technology is constantly changing and the rise in electronically communicating is becoming more and more popular, the action plan to improve patient convenience and communication should include the development of a safe software that is more secure and easily accessible for patients and their providers. With this, also come up with a way to scan daily data to re-ensure there are no viruses when sending information and that everything is running smoothly. It should include an updated hardware system, up to date software, and safe firewalls to ensure security. This is important to the organization because they're mission, vision, and values is to provide a strong foundation to make a difference.

Targeted Completion Time

This should take approximately 15 months to complete development and installation of the new systems.

Teams and Individual Responsibilities

<u>Manager Network and team members</u>: Responsible for testing the software to ensure that it is compatible with the system and devices.

Manager of Enterprise Systems: Responsible for implementing and upgrading the computer and information systems.

<u>Director of Clinical Applications</u>: Will lead the Clinical Applications team in development, implementation, and use of applications.

<u>Manager Tech Learning and Support</u>: In charge of researching the new programs and software and then pitching them to the group. Be able to support new ideas with the knowledge found during research...Should know what would work and what would not.

<u>Manager End User Platforms</u>: Responsible for delivering and explaining the services to patients or other users in a way where it is easy to understand. Also, explain things they are unaware of.

<u>The Biomed team</u>: In charge of software maintenance and ensuring the software is running smoothly at all times and if not, then repairs will be made.

Overall Goals for the IT Department

1. Enhance learning and research by using a data service that supports Essentia Health
   o Train management and staff to adopt common approaches to data issues
   o Team collaboration in order to work together, create, and solve issues through networking
   o Reduce costs and increase effectiveness
   o Design a data center services model to provide systems administration, backup, and recovery
   o Develop a disaster recovery plan
2. Develop and improve core network infrastructure
   o IT team is in charge of keeping the hardware up to date and running properly and efficiently
   o Provide wireless across Essentia Health in order for providers and other staff to access it while helping patients
3. Refine and expand systems the services are secured
   o IT will ensure the privacy, integrity, reliability, and appropriate use of information resources
   o Implement It security system in order to detect intrusion and prevent them
   o Security needs extra precautions due to patient data and the different types of networking, this could be done through the use of firewalls
   o Internet and Web need to be password protected and certain sites need to be monitored or blocked depending on the web address
4. The monitoring software must simply establish contact with the device or service using an IP address and can then retrieve the current device status.
   o Firewalls should be put in place to prevent any viruses
   o There should be security scans daily to ensure the system has no errors and is running smoothly.
5. The goal is to achieve maximum availability and optimum performance in the network. To do this, the network monitoring system must cover three security-relevant aspects:
   o monitoring the actual security systems,
   o identifying unusual occurrences, and
   o Checking environmental parameters.

6. There should be reports ran daily and updates performed weekly to ensure smooth operation and secured access to the system.
    o If there is a virus discovered then the report should be sent to the IT department Manager immediately to be resolved.
7. The software should be up to date in order for the HIM staff and providers to do their job accurately
    o Coding software should include the most up to date version and it should have all of the necessary assistance programs to go with it, this may include:
        ▪ 3M CodeAssist System
        ▪ Clinical Documentation Improvement System
        ▪ ClinTrac Software
        ▪ Electronic Signature Authentication Software

Example 4

Technology and Information Educational Services (TIES)
Information Technologies – Strategic Plan – 2016

TIES Mission

Leveraging collective wisdom to make technology work across school communities around the country in accordance with our core values: service, collaboration and innovation. (official TIES mission)

TIES Vision

As a non-profit organization, Technology and Information Educational Services will be widely regarded as a reliable partner with K-12 educators. The organization will provide software systems, professional development, and technology training for the clients, technical consulting, hardware and software support as well as ISP services. All decisions made will be in the best interest of the 48 educational districts that own TIES as well as other stakeholders. (Official TIES vision)

Information Technologies Vision

Information Technologies at TIES strives to achieve an employee-friendly environment so as to follow the core values and vision to the best of our ability as we provide our services at the highest level possible to satisfy all of our stakeholders.

Information Technologies Structure

Information Technologies at TIES is a decentralized structure. There are different decision-making levels, but every one of them relies on a team of individuals to make business decisions. It is the best structure for our organization because over the 40 years of existence we have grown significantly and are working on multiple projects simultaneously. Moreover, our decisions cannot be profit-oriented and should benefit all of our stakeholders in the first place.

Information Technologies Departmental Action Plans

Priority I: TIES will continue to follow the core values and strive to fulfil our vision.

Priority II: TIES will continue to improve its services as well as search for more educational districts across Iowa and Minnesota who could take advantage of our solutions.

Kerry (head analyst): Continue to distribute tasks and projects to teams in order to achieve the optimal development performance. Perform demos for our current and potential clients to show new functionality and discuss any changes and choose the direction the software should take. Continually, adjust direction for the EdSpring software suite to meet needs of all stakeholders efficiently. Finally, decide what each sprint should focus on.

QA Team: Continue to test our software from the user's perspective and document any broken functionality. Continually work with the Development Teams on potential ways to improve the application. Keep adding automated tests to our software suite in order to speed up the process of gathering information about the state of our software so that broken items can be fixed faster and consequently we will be able to release new features faster and more efficiently.

Blue Dev Team: Investigate changes required to migrate EdSpring suite to Meteor 1.3 and change the code base to finalize the migration by the end of August. Also, research Facebook React and Angular 2 and choose the best technology to go with Meteor 1.3 for our SaaS model of EdSpring software suite by the end of May. Continually work on assigned tasks and projects in the meantime.

Red Dev Team: Look for ways to improve the efficiency of our software by refactoring the code base. Investigate scalability potential in order to be able to serve more districts as our software suite becomes more popular. Look into changing our code standards to fit ECMAScript 2015 specification and enforce these changes by the end of the year.

Yellow Dev Team: Expand our current reporting capability in order to give users more flexibility. Investigate potential changes needed to accommodate our new database infrastructure implemented by June. Make sure that the changes will work with MongoDB 3.2 once we finish our database migration to the newest engine version.

Priority III: TIES will investigate options of upgrading our current database infrastructure and enhance the security of sensitive data about students.

Mike & Dave: Perform migration of the database engine to MongoDB 3.2 by June. This task should also take care of optimizing as many time intensive queries as possible to improve the overall performance of our software. Continually look into ways of improving the security of sensitive student personal data to comply with new regulations. Work on improving the process of SIF imports to our Student Information System since users reported extremely slow software performance during import intensive periods.

QA Team: Collaborate with NEUSTAR on load testing for our software to see how the planned changes to our application affect the scalability of the platform. Create a report of any issues that come out in the process by the end of July so the Dev Teams have time to fix them before new academic year begins.

Example 5
Information Technologies – Strategic Plan – 2007/2008

College Mission

Shaped by the Catholic Benedictine heritage, The College of St. Scholastica provides intellectual and moral preparation for responsible living and meaningful work.

College Vision

The College of St. Scholastica will be widely regarded as an academic community grounded in the rich Benedictine heritage and sending forth thoughtful leaders, sharpened and sensitized by the liberal arts, who are committed to serve and to transform the world.

Information Technologies Vision

Information Technologies fosters an environment that promotes and enhances the College's vision and exemplifies its Benedictine values as we provide the technologies to be adaptable, efficient, competitive, and forward thinking; while remaining fiscally responsible as we serve students, faculty and staff.

Information Technologies
Departmental Action Plans

Priority I: The College will preserve, highlight, and observe its mission and heritage.

Priority II: The College will encourage and reward bold and creative thinking, flexibility, and accountability.

Mark P & AC Group: Continue to implement the Business Intelligence System. Work with appropriate managers and data owners to:
- Migrate routine data inquiry and reporting applications from our homegrown MS Access data warehouses to the BANNER Operational Data Store (ODS)
- Develop at least two cubes for financial and enrollment reporting in the Enterprise Data Warehouse (EDW) environment.
- Develop at least two academic reports for course enrollments and faculty load.
- Begin to migrate appropriate MS Access applications to the .net environment
- Upgrade Cognos to version 8

Tech Services: As part of the College's Title III grant, continue to work with the ATHENS project to integrate CERNER Medical Software into the College's Health Sciences curriculum through the roll out of additional state of the art technologies that facilitate the objectives of the grant through October 2007.
Lynne: Collaborate with the School of Nursing and the School of Health Sciences to transition the ATHENS project from grant funding to institutional support by October 2007.

Priority III: To address the needs of traditional and non-traditional learners, the College will strive for the highest quality in its academic programs and student services.

Will/Mike L: Expand Internet connectivity (increase bandwidth) by 10 MB to continue to meet the increasing bandwidth needs of our students and academic activities by September 2007. Continually research alternative technologies to provide the most cost effective and scalable solution to meet the needs for the College's administrative and ResNet networks over the next three years.

John: Continue the technology classroom plan by upgrading 8 classrooms with the networked classroom control systems by September 2007. This system provides a customer friendly user interface for faculty, more functionality for additional technologies, the ability to provide more efficient help desk support, and security for classroom equipment.

John & Sarah: Research, recommend, and implement videoconferencing and web conferencing solutions that will enhance our ability to create and provide an outstanding digital learning environment to existing and future markets by May 2008.

Sarah: The Academic Technology Plan will address the need to develop a referral and support mechanism to ensure that students have the technology expertise needed to succeed in both traditional/classroom and online learning environments. Components of this plan will involve participation from many areas including Academic Advisement, IT User Services, IT Technical Services, IT Web Services, and Faculty.

Web Team: Design, test and implement web templates for mobile technologies such as PDA's and cell phones to meet the information needs of our students by June 2008.

<u>Priority IV</u>: The College will develop a competitive physical infrastructure to attract students and support learning.

Lowell: Plan, test, and roll-out the migration to Office 07 by August 2007. This will include coordination with network services, user services for training and documentation, and end users for testing.

Will & Network Services: Implement the first year of the multi-year ubiquitous wireless networking plan with the intent to ensure the entire campus, including residence halls, apartments, and outside common areas, have wireless access by May 2008.

Example 6
Information Technologies - Strategic Plan - 2016/2017

Twitter's Mission

Twitter aims to give everyone the power to create and share ideas and information instantly, without barriers.

Twitter's Vision

Twitter seeks to reach the largest daily audience in the world by connecting everyone to their world via our information sharing and distribution platform products and be one of the top revenue generating Internet companies in the world.

Information Technologies Vision

Information Technologies fosters an environment that promotes and enhances Twitter's vision and exemplifies our mission statement as we provide the technologies to be adaptable, efficient, and forward thinking; while remaining responsible as we serve people around the world.

Information Technologies
Departmental Action Plans

Goal I: Twitter allows users to promote, share, and receive a large amount of data and trending topics from around the world.
Continue to implement the Business Intelligence System. Work with appropriate managers and data owners to:
- Migrate routine data inquiry and reporting applications from our warehouses
- Begin to migrate appropriate MS Access applications to the .net environment
  1. The ability to share and receive large amounts of data is important to Twitter because data is one of the most valuable commodities for the company.
  2. Target Completion Date: 2-4 weeks
  3. Individual(s) responsible for project completion: Emily and Dan

Goal II: Twitter needs a reliable server systems that can handle the large amounts of traffic and be able to store the data.
- Research, purchase and install a server system for the primary purpose of server storage consolidation. This will allow us to use disk space more efficiently and also to get the most out of our software.
  1. The goal for updating Twitter's server system is to potentially improve reliability of data storage and user experience. This could be done multiple times a year if needed as Twitter gains more popularity.
  2. Target Completion Date: 6-12 months
  3. Individual(s) responsible for project completion: Abby, Larry, and Sam

Goal III: Twitter relies on the latest version of software to solve any software bugs and to allow for new services and features that their customers can enjoy.
- Update to the newest software or use an open source program to manually edit Twitter's interface. This ensures that the website is running smoothly and meeting users' requests and suggestions for improvements

1. The goal for updating Twitter's software is to provide the most up-to-date programs that have new services and features for customers, and get rid of any bugs that may be affecting the software's performance.
2. Target Completion Date: 3-6 months
3. Individual(s) responsible for project completion: Tom, Clark, Leah, and Ron

Goal IV: Twitter's website requires enough bandwidth to support 320 million users and 1 billion unique visitors.
*   Expand Internet connectivity (increase bandwidth) by 5 GB to continue to meet the increasing bandwidth needs of our users and visitors.
    1. The goal for updating Twitter's network is to allow access for existing users and new visitors and provide fast service.
    2. Target Completion Date: 3-4 weeks
    3. Individual(s) responsible for project completion: Nicole, Brandon, and Roger

Goal V: Twitter needs to have the most up-to-date security to ensure that user information and accounts are secured and protected against cyberattacks.
*   Improve current security system to a more reliable and easy to understand interface for developers to insure a strong firewall in the server system.
    1. The goal for updating Twitter's security will ensure that all user's information is secure from hackers and other malicious third party applications. This will yield a high user satisfaction rate knowing that their accounts are secured by Twitter's high end security system.
    2. Target Completion Date: 2-3 months
    3. Individual(s) responsible for project completion: Sarah, Connie, and Jim

Goal VI: Twitter needs a strong and reliable Internet and Web connection to ensure the connectivity of all users.
*   Change to a more reliable internet provider that can sufficiently handle the website's needs. This will allow the website to have more megabits per second ensuring Twitter's data is being shared quickly and efficiently
    1. The goal for updating Twitter's internet is to give the site a reliable internet connection preventing any website crashes or freezing. Users want to have a fast site to continually update and share tweets.
    2. Target Completion Date: 3-4 weeks
    3. Individual(s) responsible for project completion: Nathan, Zach, and Katharine

Goal VII: Twitter needs an effective reporting system that allows issues to get marked as soon as possible.
*   The most important part of ensuring users' satisfaction is making sure that bugs or crashes are reported by users to be sent to the developers. This allows developers to fix errors and problems within the website, servers and internet connection.
    1. The goal for reporting is allowing users to easily access the page to report errors. This should also encourage users to report the problems they are having to ensure that every Twitter user has the best experience possible.
    2. Target Completion Date: 1 month
    3. Individual(s) responsible for project completion: Bob, Bethany, Bert and Connor

THOMAS L BUCK

STAGE 2 - SWOT ANALYSIS QUESTIONNAIRE

CONDUCTING A SWOT ANALYSIS:
Example Questions

A strategic analysis of the organization and the external environment will enable the organization to plan more effectively for the future, whilst taking into account opportunities and potential threats. The following key questions provide a basis for this analysis.

What are your organization's strengths and weaknesses? *For example:*

- **What are your main achievements over the last three years?**

- **How successful have you been in achieving your strategic objectives?**

- **Have you met or exceeded your targets?**

- **Do your current services meet users' requirements?**

- **How effective are your links with other key organizations/agencies in your area or sector?**

- **How secure is your organization's financial position?**

- **Do you have the staff/volunteer levels and expertise necessary to meet your objectives?**

- **How is your organization regarded externally? Does it have a good reputation? Are you able to build effective relationships with those you wish to influence? Do you have a positive relationship with your funders/supporters?**

- **Is your organization effective at communicating with external groups?**

- **How effective are your management systems and processes? Is your organization well-structured and efficient or overly bureaucratic?**

- **Does your IT Department have the capacity/expertise to meet the demands of the organization?**

What are the key opportunities and threats facing your organization? *You may wish to consider, for example:*

- **Trends in your area of work/services**

- **Audit of local situation**

- **Membership / user needs**

- **Demographics**

- **Competition from other or similar organizations in your area**

- **Facilities**

- **Barriers to your organization's development**

- **Deprivation of your catchment area e.g. Noble Deprivation Indices**

- **Consultation findings, e.g. community audit, need assessment, etc.**

- **Opportunities for developing new area of work**

- **Opportunities for extending services to new audiences**

- **Partnerships / collaborative working opportunities**

- **Local authority policies and plans in your area**

- **Education and Library Board policies and plans**

- **Health and Social Service Board policies and plans**

- **Other policy documents relevant to you organization's work or location, e.g. Taskforce**

- **Funding opportunities for your organization**

THOMAS L BUCK

STAGE 2 - SWOT ANALYSIS WORKSHEET

SWOT ANALYSIS WORKSHEET
Where are we now?

	Strengths	Weaknesses
INTERNAL Environment		
EXTERNAL Environment	Opportunities	Threats

STAGE 2 - DEVELOPING DEPARTMENT VALUES WORKSHEET

DEVELOPING ORGANIZATIONAL VALUES

The ethos of your organization is the set of beliefs and principles that guide your work. Other terms for ethos are the philosophy or values of an organization.

The values of your organization will guide all aspects of your programs and activities in terms of principle and practice.

Exercise:

1.   Word-storm:

     What guiding principles are important to:

     - How your organization operates (e.g. its activities, standards, quality, etc.
     - How your organization is perceived externally (i.e. in the eyes of the public or other external stakeholders)
     - How staff and volunteers carry out your organization's services and activities?

2.   Discuss and agree whether your organization needs a shared value base in order to operate more effectively.

3.   If so, agree at least 5 values that are appropriate for your organization.

STAGE 2 - DEVELOPING A MISSION STATEMENT WORKSHEET

DEVELOPING A MISSION STATEMENT

The mission statement is:

- The core message of the organization's purpose and reason it exists;
- What you are trying to do, why, and for whom.

Exercise 1:

In one or two sentences, describe the overall purpose of the organisation in a way that looks to your vision and says what you're trying to do and for whom.

Exercise 2:

Review the objects statement of the organization (this will be found in your constitution or memorandum/articles), and answer the following:

- How do your "objects" relate to the overall purpose and mission of the organisation over the next 3-5 years?

Use this as a basis for reviewing / writing a mission statement.

Shaped by the Catholic Benedictine heritage, The College of St. Scholastica provides intellectual and moral preparation for responsible living and meaningful work.

STAGE 2 - DEVELOPING A VISION STATEMENT WORKSHEET

DEVELOPING A VISION STATEMENT

A vision is a clear and inspirational hope for the future.

Exercise 1:

In one sentence, describe the long-term change that you would like to see brought about in an ideal world, as a result of your organization's work.

Exercise 2: "map your vision"

In small groups - on a large piece of paper, draw a picture or diagram of what your organization would be like if it was doing everything you think it should be doing and had all the resources it needed.

Share your ideas with the other groups. Points for discussion:

- Are the groups of one mind? What are the differences?
- Is there a collective picture of the organization's vision? If not, can one be agreed?

Sample: Information Technologies fosters an environment that promotes and enhances the College's vision and exemplifies its Benedictine values as we provide the technologies to be adaptable, efficient, competitive, and forward thinking; while remaining fiscally responsible as we serve students. faculty and staff.

STAGE 3 - PRIORITIES AND STRATEGIC AIMS WORKSHEET

PRIORITIES AND STRATEGIC AIMS

Strategic aims set out priority areas of work for an organization. Your strategic aims should:

- Help achieve your mission (overall purpose)
- Be limited in number (i.e. 4 to 10)
- Show clear direction

Exercise:

1. From your SWOT analysis and review of achievements, make a list of themed priority areas of work for your organization. (1 or 2 words only)

    Example: Training
    Community Development
    Capacity Building
    Income Generation

2. Does the list of key words fit with your organization's core purpose/mission? Can these key words form the basis of your long-term aims?

3. From your SWOT analysis, are there opportunities / new areas of work that fit your mission, and should be included in your long-term aims?

4. Finalise your list of priority areas of work for the next 3 years.

THOMAS L BUCK

STAGE 3 - EXAMPLE STRATEGIC AIMS

EXAMPLE
Strategic Aims

1. **Community Development**
   Aim: To promote good practice in community development through education and training.

2. **Participation and Consultation**
   Aim: To build and sustain a relationship with our members and their local community which is constructive, effective and mutually valued.

3. **Research**
   Aim: To support research which will contribute to the achievement of the organization's mission.

4. **Campaigning**
   Aim: To help shape the future of public policy and statutory services.

5. **Finance and Resources**
   Aim: To have an integrated system for the regular planning and reviewing of organizational resources and funding to achieve its aims and objectives.

6. **Policy**
   Aim: To influence public policy, creating a greater awareness and understanding of the role of volunteering in strengthening civil society and building social capital.

7. **Members, Volunteers and Staff**
   Aim: Members, volunteers and staff have the skills and support they need to fulfil the organization's mission, aims and objectives effectively.

EXAMPLE
Strategic Aims (Rural Community Network)

Aim 1	**Empowering the voice of rural communities** To provide rural people with the skills required to engage effectively with decision makers.
Aim 2	**Championing excellence in rural community development practice** To promote rural community development practice as an agent for change.
Aim 3	**Developing civic leadership in rural communities** To promote volunteering and, in particular, focus on encouraging volunteers from the most excluded sectors of rural society.
Aim 4	**Actively working towards an equitable and peaceful society** To support rural communities in making a contribution towards 'a Shared Future' through community relations and good relations work.
Aim 5	**Promoting the sustainable development of rural communities** To support rural communities in exploring what sustainable

STAGES 3 & 4 - STRATEGIC OBJECTIVES WORKSHEET

STRATEGIC OBJECTIVES

Strategic objectives give an idea of key activities (key areas of work) that are required to achieve each long-term, strategic aim. You may wish to refer back to your SWOT at this stage, to check that all factors (both internal and external) that may have a bearing on your objectives have been taken into account.

Exercise:

Consider each **long-term aim** and list up to 6 activities that will:

a)   Have the greatest impact

1. _____
2. _____
3. _____
4. _____
5. _____
6. _____

b)   Make best use of resources

1. _____
2. _____
3. _____
4. _____
5. _____
6. _____

c)   Help achieve the aim (and hence the organization's mission)

1. _____
2. _____
3. _____
4. _____
5. _____
6. _____

Strategic objectives are different than operational objectives. Operational objectives give more detailed instructions that will feed into work plans and day-to-day operations.

COMPUTER INFORMATION SYSTEMS GLOSSARY

A

Acceptance Testing: Provides the final certification that the system is ready to be used in a production setting.

Access Control: Policies and procedures to prevent improper access to systems.

Access Point: Box consisting of a radio receiver/transmitter and antennae that link to a wired network, router, or hub.

Accountability: The mechanisms for assessing responsibility for decisions made and actions taken.

Accounting Rate Of Return On Investment (ROI): Calculation of the rate of return on an investment by adjusting cash inflows produced by the investment for depreciation. Approximates the accounting income earned by the investment.

Accumulated Balance Digital Payment Systems: Systems enabling users to make micropayments and purchases on the Web, accumulating a debit balance on their credit card or telephone bills.

Activity-Based Costing: Model for identifying all the company activities that cause costs to occur while producing a specific product or service so that managers can see which products or services are profitable or losing money and make changes to maximize firm profitability.

Administrative Controls: Formalized standards, rules, procedures, and disciplines to ensure that the organization's controls are properly executed and enforced.

Agency Theory: Economic theory that views the firm as a nexus of contracts among self-interested individuals who must be supervised and managed.

AI Shell: The programming environment of an expert system.

analog signal: A continuous waveform that passes through a communications medium; used for voice communications.

Analytical CRM: Customer relationship management applications dealing with the analysis of customer data to provide information for improving business performance.

Application Controls: Specific controls unique to each computerized application.

Application Server: Software that handles all application operations between browser-based computers and a company's back-end business applications or databases.

Application Service Provider (ASP): Company providing software that can be rented by other companies over the Web or a private network.

Application Software Package: A set of prewritten, precoded application software programs that are commercially available for sale or lease.

Application Software: Programs written for a specific application to perform functions specified by end users.

Arithmetic-Logic Unit (ALU): Component of the CPU that performs the computer's principal logic and arithmetic operations.

Artificial Intelligence (AI): The effort to develop computer-based systems that can behave like humans, with the ability to learn languages, accomplish physical tasks, use a perceptual apparatus, and emulate human expertise and decision making.

Asynchronous Transfer Mode (ATM): A networking technology that parcels information into 8-byte cells, allowing data to be transmitted between computers from different vendors at any speed.

Attribute: A piece of information describing a particular entity.

Authentication: The ability of each party in a transaction to ascertain the identity of the other party.

Automation: Using the computer to speed up the performance of existing tasks.

B

Backbone: Part of a network handling the major traffic and providing the primary path for traffic flowing to or from other networks.

Backward Chaining: A strategy for searching the rule base in an expert system that acts like a problem solver by beginning with a hypothesis and seeking out more information until the hypothesis is either proved or disproved.

Balanced Scorecard: Model for analyzing firm performance which supplements traditional financial measures with measurements from additional business perspectives, such as customers, internal business processes, and learning and growth.

Bandwidth: The capacity of a communications channel as measured by the difference between the highest and lowest frequencies that can be transmitted by that channel.

Banner Ad: A graphic display on a Web page used for advertising. The banner is linked to the advertiser's Web site so that a person clicking on it will be transported to the advertiser's Web site.

Batch Processing: A method of collecting and processing data in which transactions are accumulated and stored until a specified time when it is convenient or necessary to process them as a group.

Baud: A change in signal from positive to negative or vice versa that is used as a measure of transmission speed.

Behavioral Models: Descriptions of management based on behavioral scientists' observations of what managers actually do in their jobs.

Benchmarking: Setting strict standards for products, services, or activities and measuring organizational performance against those standards.

Best Practices: The most successful solutions or problem-solving methods that have been developed by a specific organization or industry.

Biometric Authentication: Technology for authenticating system users that compares a person's unique characteristics such as fingerprints, face, or retinal image, against a stored set profile of these characteristics.

Bit: A binary digit representing the smallest unit of data in a computer system. It can only have one of two states, representing 0 or 1.

Bluetooth: Standard for wireless personal area networks that can transmit up to 722 Kbps within a 10-meter area.

Broadband: High-speed transmission technology. Also designates a single communications medium that can transmit multiple channels of data simultaneously.

Bugs: Program code defects or errors.

Bullwhip Effect: Distortion of information about the demand for a product as it passes from one entity to the next across the supply chain.

Bundling: Cross-selling in which a combination of products is sold as a bundle at a price lower than the total cost of the individual products.

Bureaucracy: Formal organization with a clear-cut division of labor, abstract rules and procedures, and impartial decision making that uses technical qualifications and professionalism as a basis for promoting employees.

Bureaucratic Models Of Decision Making: Models of decision making where decisions are shaped by the organization's standard operating procedures (SOPs).

bus network: Network topology linking a number of computers by a single circuit with all messages broadcast to the entire network.

Business Continuity Planning: Planning that focuses on how the company can restore business operations after a disaster strikes.

Business Functions: Specialized tasks performed in a business organization, including manufacturing and production, sales and marketing, finance and accounting, and human resources.

Business Intelligence: Applications and technologies that focus on gathering, storing, analyzing, and providing access to data from many different sources to help users make better business decisions.

Business Model: An abstraction of what an enterprise is and how the enterprise delivers a product or service, showing how the enterprise creates wealth.

Business Process Management: Methodology for revising the organization's business processes to use business processes as fundamental building blocks of corporate information systems.

Business Process Reengineering: The radical redesign of business processes, combining steps to cut waste and eliminating repetitive, paper-intensive tasks in order to improve cost, quality, and service, and to maximize the benefits of information technology.

Business Processes: The unique ways in which organizations coordinate and organize work activities, information, and knowledge to produce a product or service.

Business-To-Business (B2B) Electronic Commerce: Electronic sales of goods and services among businesses.

Business-To-Consumer (B2C) Electronic Commerce: Electronic retailing of products and services directly to individual consumers.

Byte: A string of bits, usually eight, used to store one number or character in a computer system.

C

C: A powerful programming language with tight control and efficiency of execution; is portable across different microprocessors and is used primarily with PCs.

C++: Object-oriented version of the C programming language.

Cable Modem: Modem designed to operate over cable TV lines to provide high-speed access to the Web or corporate intranets.

Call Center: An organizational department responsible for handling customer service issues by telephone and other channels.

Capacity Planning: The process of predicting when a computer hardware system becomes saturated to ensure that adequate computing resources are available for work of different priorities and that the firm has enough computing power for its current and future needs.

Capital Budgeting: The process of analyzing and selecting various proposals for capital expenditures.

Carpal Tunnel Syndrome (CTS): Type of RSI in which pressure on the median nerve through the wrist's bony carpal tunnel structure produces pain.

Case-Based Reasoning (CBR): Artificial intelligence technology that represents knowledge as a database of cases and solutions.

Centralized Processing: Processing that is accomplished by one large central computer.

Change Agent: In the context of implementation, the individual acting as the catalyst during the change process to ensure successful organizational adaptation to a new system or innovation.

Channel Conflict: Competition between two or more different distribution chains used to sell the products or services of the same company.

Channel: The link by which data or voice are transmitted between sending and receiving devices in a network.

Chief Information Officer (CIO): Senior manager in charge of the information systems function in the firm.

Chief Knowledge Officer (CKO): Senior executive in charge of the organization's knowledge management program.

Choice: Simon's third stage of decision making, when the individual selects among the various solution alternatives.

Churn Rate: Measurement of the number of customers who stop using or purchasing products or services from a company. Used as an indicator of the growth or decline of a firm's customer base.

Classical Model Of Management: Traditional description of management that focused on its formal functions of planning, organizing, coordinating, deciding, and controlling.

Clicks-And-Mortar: Business model where the Web site is an extension of a traditional bricks-and-mortar business.

Clickstream Tracking: Tracking data about customer activities at Web sites and storing them in a log.

Client: The user point-of-entry for the required function in client/server computing. Normally a desktop computer, workstation, or laptop computer.

Client/Server Computing: A model for computing that splits processing between clients and servers on a network, assigning functions to the machine most able to perform the function.

Clustering: Linking two computers together so that the second computer can act as a backup to the primary computer or speed up processing.

COBOL (COmmon Business Oriented Language): Major programming language for business applications because it can process large data files with alphanumeric characters.

Cognitive Style: Underlying personality dispositions toward the treatment of information, selection of alternatives, and evaluation of consequences.

Collaborative Commerce: The use of digital technologies to enable multiple organizations to collaboratively design, develop, build and manage products through their life cycles.

Collaborative Filtering: Tracking users' movements on a Web site, comparing the information gleaned about a user's behavior against data about other customers with similar interests to predict what the user would like to see next.

Collaborative Planning, Forecasting, And Replenishment (CPFR): Firms collaborating with their suppliers and buyers to formulate demand forecasts, develop production plans, and coordinate shipping, warehousing, and stocking activities.

Communications Technology: Physical devices and software that link various computer hardware components and transfer data from one physical location to another.

Competitive Forces Model: Model used to describe the interaction of external influences, specifically threats and opportunities, that affect an organization's strategy and ability to compete.

Compiler: Special system software that translates a high-level language into machine language for execution by the computer.

Complementary Assets: Additional assets required to derive value from a primary investment.

Component-Based Development: Building large software systems by combining pre-existing software components.

Computer Forensics: The scientific collection, examination, authentication, preservation, and analysis of data held on or retrieved from computer storage media in such a way that the information can be used as evidence in a court of law.

Computer-Aided Design (CAD): Information system that automates the creation and revision of designs using sophisticated graphics software.

Computer-Aided Software Engineering (CASE): Automation of step-by-step methodologies for software and systems development to reduce the amounts of repetitive work the developer needs to do.

Computer-Based Information Systems (CBIS): Information systems that rely on computer hardware and software for processing and disseminating information.

Conceptual Schema: The logical description of the entire database showing all the data elements and relationships among them.

Connectivity: The ability of computers and computer-based devices to communicate with each other and share information in a meaningful way without human intervention..

Consumer-To-Consumer (C2C): electronic commerce Consumers selling goods and services electronically to other consumers.

Control Unit: Component of the CPU that controls and coordinates the other parts of the computer system.

Controls: All of the methods, policies, and procedures that ensure protection of the organization's assets, accuracy and reliability of its records, and operational adherence to management standards.

Converged Network: Network with technology to enable voice and data to run over a single network.

Conversion: The process of changing from the old system to the new system.

Cooptation: Bringing the opposition into the process of designing and implementing a solution without giving up control of the direction and nature of the change.

Core Competency: Activity at which a firm excels as a world-class leader.

Core Systems: Systems that support functions that are absolutely critical to the organization.

Cost-Benefit Ratio: A method for calculating the returns from a capital expenditure by dividing total benefits by total costs.

Counterimplementation: A deliberate strategy to thwart the implementation of an information system or an innovation in an organization.

Critical Success Factors (Csfs): A small number of easily identifiable operational goals shaped by the industry, the firm, the manager, and the broader environment that are believed to assure the success of an organization. Used to determine the information requirements of an organization.

Cross-Selling: Marketing complementary products to customers.

Customer-Decision-Support System (CDSS): System to support the decision-making process of an existing or potential customer.

Customer Lifetime Value (CLTV): Difference between revenues produced by a specific customer and the expenses for acquiring and servicing that customer minus the cost of promotional marketing over the lifetime of the customer relationship, expressed in today's dollars.

Customer Relationship Management (CRM): Business and technology discipline that uses information systems to coordinate all of the business processes surrounding the firm's interactions with its customers in sales, marketing, and service.

Customer Relationship Management Systems: Information systems that track all the ways in which a company interacts with its customers and analyze these interactions to optimize revenue, profitability, customer satisfaction, and customer retention.

Customization: The modification of a software package to meet an organization's unique requirements without destroying the package software's integrity.

D

Data: Streams of raw facts representing events occurring in organizations or the physical environment before they have been organized and arranged into a form that people can understand and use.

Data Administration: A special organizational function for managing the organization's data resources, concerned with information policy, data planning, maintenance of data dictionaries, and data quality standards.

Data Definition Language: The component of a database management system that defines each data element as it appears in the database.

Data Dictionary: An automated or manual tool for storing and organizing information about the data maintained in a database.

Data-Driven DSS: A system that supports decision making by allowing users to extract and analyze useful information that was previously buried in large databases.

Data Element: A field.

Data Flow Diagram (DFD): Primary tool for structured analysis that graphically illustrates a system's component process and the flow of data between them.

Data Inconsistency: The presence of different values for same attribute when the same data are stored in multiple locations.

Data Management Software: Software used for creating and manipulating lists, creating files and databases to store data, and combining information for reports.

Data Manipulation Language: A language associated with a database management system that end users and programmers use to manipulate data in the database.

Data Mart: A small data warehouse containing only a portion of the organization's data for a specified function or population of users.

Data Quality Audit: A survey and/or sample of files to determine accuracy and completeness of data in an information system.

Data Redundancy: The presence of duplicate data in multiple data files.

Data Security Controls: Controls to ensure that data files on either disk or tape are not subject to unauthorized access, change, or destruction.

Data Visualization: Technology for helping users see patterns and relationships in large amounts of data by presenting the data in graphical form.

Data Warehouse: A database, with reporting and query tools, that stores current and historical data extracted from various operational systems and consolidated for management reporting and analysis.

Data Workers: People such as secretaries or bookkeepers who process the organization's paperwork.

Database: A group of related files.

Database (Rigorous Definition): A collection of data organized to service many applications at the same time by storing and managing data so that they appear to be in one location.

Database Administration: Refers to the more technical and operational aspects of managing data, including physical database design and maintenance.

Database Management System (DBMS): Special software to create and maintain a database and enable individual business applications to extract the data they need without having to create separate files or data definitions in their computer programs.

Database Server: A computer in a client/server environment that is responsible for running a DBMS to process SQL statements and perform database management tasks.

Dataconferencing: Teleconferencing in which two or more users are able to edit and modify data files simultaneously.

Datamining: Analysis of large pools of data to find patterns and rules that can be used to guide decision making and predict future behavior.

Debugging: The process of discovering and eliminating the errors and defects--bugs--in program code.

Decisional Roles: Mintzberg's classification for managerial roles where managers initiate activities, handle disturbances, allocate resources, and negotiate conflicts.

Decision-Support Systems (DSS): Information systems at the organization's management level that combine data and sophisticated analytical models or data analysis tools to support semistructured and unstructured decision making.

Dedicated Lines: Telephone lines that are continuously available for transmission by a lessee. Typically conditioned to transmit data at high speeds for high-volume applications.

Demand Planning: Determining how much product a business needs to make to satisfy all its customers' demands.

Denial Of Service (Dos) Attack: Flooding a network server or Web server with false communications or requests for services in order to crash the network.

Dense Wave Division Multiplexing (DWDM): Technology for boosting transmission capacity of optical fiber by using many different wavelengths to carry separate streams of data over the same fiber strand at the same time.

Descartes' Rule Of Change: A principle that states that if an action cannot be taken repeatedly, then it is not right to be taken at any time.

Design: Simon's second stage of decision making, when the individual conceives of possible alternative solutions to a problem.

Development Methodology: A collection of methods, one or more for every activity within every phase of a development project.

Digital Divide: Large disparities in access to computers and the Internet among different social groups and different locations.

Digital Firm: Organization where nearly all significant business processes and relationships with customers, suppliers, and employees are digitally enabled, and key corporate assets are managed through digital means.

Digital Market: A marketplace that is created by computer and communication technologies that link many buyers and sellers.

Digital Millennium Copyright Act (DMCA): Adjusts copyright laws to the Internet Age by making it illegal to make, distribute, or use devices that circumvent technology-based protections of copy-righted materials.

Digital Signal: A discrete waveform that transmits data coded into two discrete states as 1-bits and 0-bits, which are represented as on-off electrical pulses; used for data communications.

Digital Signature: A digital code that can be attached to an electronically transmitted message to uniquely identify its contents and the sender.

Digital Subscriber Line (DSL): A group of technologies providing high-capacity transmission over existing copper telephone lines.

Digital Video Disk (DVD): High-capacity optical storage medium that can store full-length videos and large amounts of data.

Digital Wallet: Software that stores credit card, electronic cash, owner identification, and address information and provides this data automatically during electronic commerce purchase transactions.

Direct Cutover: A risky conversion approach where the new system completely replaces the old one on an appointed day.

Disaster Recovery Planning: Planning for the restoration of computing and communications services after they have been disrupted.

Disintermediation: The removal of organizations or business process layers responsible for certain intermediary steps in a value chain.

Distance Learning: Education or training delivered over a distance to individuals in one or more locations.

Distributed Database: A database that is stored in more than one physical location. Parts or copies of the database are physically stored in one location, and other parts or copies are stored and maintained in other locations.

Distributed Processing: The distribution of computer processing work among multiple computers linked by a communications network.

Documentation: Descriptions of how an information system works from either a technical or end-user standpoint.

Domain Name: The name identifying a unique node on the Internet.

Domain Name System (DNS): A hierarchical system of servers maintaining database enabling the conversion of domain names to their IP addresses.

Domestic Exporter: Form of business organization characterized by heavy centralization of corporate activities in the home country of origin.

Downsizing: The process of transferring applications from large computers to smaller ones.

Downtime: Period of time in which an information system is not operational.

Drill Down: The ability to move from summary data to lower and lower levels of detail.

DSS Database: A collection of current or historical data from a number of applications or groups. Can be a small PC database or a massive data warehouse.

DSS Software System: Collection of software tools that are used for data analysis, such as OLAP tools, datamining tools, or a collection of mathematical and analytical models.

Due Process: A process in which laws are well-known and understood and there is an ability to appeal to higher authorities to ensure that laws are applied correctly.

Dynamic Page Generation: Technology for storing the contents of Web pages as objects in a database where they can be accessed and assembled to create constantly changing Web pages.

Dynamic Pricing: Pricing of items based on real-time interactions between buyers and sellers that determine what an item is worth at any particular moment.

E

e-Business: The use of the Internet and digital technology to execute all the business processes in the enterprise. Includes e-commerce as well as processes for the internal management of the firm and for coordination with suppliers and other business partners.

e-Commerce: Commercial transactions conducted electronically on the Internet.

e-Government: Use of the Internet and related technologies to digitally enable government and public sector agencies' relationships with citizens, businesses, and other arms of government.

e-Learning: Instruction delivered through purely digital technology, such as CD-ROMs, the Internet, or private networks.

e-Marketing: Refers to advertising and marketing efforts that use the Web and email to drive direct sales via electronic commerce, in addition to sales leads from Web sites or emails.

Efficient Customer Response System: System that directly links consumer behavior back to distribution, production, and supply chains.

Electronic Billing And Payment Presentation System: Systems used for paying routine monthly bills that allow users to view their bills electronically and pay them through electronic funds transfers from banks or credit card accounts.

Electronic Commerce Server Software: Software that provides functions essential for running e-commerce Web sites, such as setting up electronic catalogs and storefronts, and mechanisms for processing customer purchases.

Electronic Data Interchange (EDI): The direct computer-to-computer exchange between two organizations of standard business transaction documents.

Encryption: The coding and scrambling of messages to prevent their being read or accessed without authorization.

End Users: Representatives of departments outside the information systems group for whom applications are developed.

End-User Development: The development of information systems by end users with little or no formal assistance from technical specialists.

End-User Interface: The part of an information system through which the end user interacts with the system, such as on-line screens and commands.

Enterprise Analysis: An analysis of organization-wide information requirements by looking at the entire organization in terms of organizational units, functions, processes, and data elements; helps identify the key entities and attributes in the organization's data.

Enterprise Applications: Systems that can coordinate activities, decisions, and knowledge across many different functions, levels, and business units in a firm. Include enterprise systems, supply chain management systems, and knowledge management systems.

Enterprise Application Integration (EAI) Software: Software that works with specific software platforms to tie together multiple applications to support enterprise integration.

Enterprise Networking: An arrangement of the organization's hardware, software, network, and data resources to put more computing power on the desktop and create a company-wide network linking many smaller networks.

Enterprise Portal: Web interface providing a single entry point for accessing organizational information and services, including information from various enterprise applications and in-house legacy systems so that information appears to be coming from a single source.

Enterprise Software: Set of integrated modules for applications such as sales and distribution, financial accounting, investment management, materials management, production planning, plant maintenance, and human resources that allow data to be used by multiple functions and business processes.

Enterprise Systems: Integrated enterprise-wide information systems that coordinate key internal processes of the firm.

Entity: A person, place, thing, or event about which information must be kept.

Entity-Relationship Diagram: A methodology for documenting databases illustrating the relationship between various entities in the database.

Ergonomics: The interaction of people and machines in the work environment, including the design of jobs, health issues, and the end-user interface of information systems.

Ethical "No Free Lunch" Rule: Assumption that all tangible and intangible objects are owned by someone else, unless there is a specific declaration otherwise, and that the creator wants compensation for this work.

Ethics: Principles of right and wrong that can be used by individuals acting as free moral agents to make choices to guide their behavior.

Exchange: Third-party Net marketplace that is primarily transaction oriented and that connects many buyers and suppliers for spot purchasing.

Executive Support Systems (ESS): Information systems at the organization's strategic level designed to address unstructured decision making through advanced graphics and communications.

Expert System: Knowledge-intensive computer program that captures the expertise of a human in limited domains of knowledge.

Explicit Knowledge: Knowledge that has been documented.

External Integration Tools: Project management technique that links the work of the implementation team to that of users at all organizational levels.

Extranet: Private intranet that is accessible to authorized outsiders.

F

Fair Information Practices (FIP): A set of principles originally set forth in 1973 that governs the collection and use of information about individuals and forms the basis of most U.S. and European privacy laws.

Fault-Tolerant Computer Systems: Systems that contain extra hardware, software, and power supply components that can back a system up and keep it running to prevent system failure.

Feasibility Study: As part of the systems analysis process, the way to determine whether the solution is achievable, given the organization's resources and constraints.

Feedback: Output that is returned to the appropriate members of the organization to help them evaluate or correct input.

Fiber-Optic Cable: A fast, light, and durable transmission medium consisting of thin strands of clear glass fiber bound into cables. Data are transmitted as light pulses.

Field: A grouping of characters into a word, a group of words, or a complete number, such as a person's name or age.

Finance And Accounting Information Systems: Systems keep track of the firm's financial assets and fund flows.

Focused Differentiation: Competitive strategy for developing new market niches for specialized products or services where a business can compete in the target area better than its competitors.

Formal Control Tools: Project management technique that helps monitor the progress toward completion of a task and fulfillment of goals.

Formal Planning Tools: Project management technique that structures and sequences tasks, budgeting time, money, and technical resources required to complete the tasks.

Formal System: System resting on accepted and fixed definitions of data and procedures, operating with predefined rules.

Forward Chaining: A strategy for searching the rule base in an expert system that begins with the information entered by the user and searches the rule base to arrive at a conclusion.

Fourth-Generation Language: A programming language that can be employed directly by end users or less-skilled programmers to develop computer applications more rapidly than conventional programming languages.

Frame Relay: A shared network service technology that packages data into bundles for transmission but does not use error-correction routines. Cheaper and faster than packet switching.

Framing: Displaying the content of another Web site inside one's own Web site within a frame or a window.

Franchiser: Form of business organization in which a product is created, designed, financed, and initially produced in the home country, but for product-specific reasons relies heavily on foreign personnel for further production, marketing, and human resources.

Fuzzy Logic: Rule-based AI that tolerates imprecision by using nonspecific terms called membership functions to solve problems.

G

"Garbage Can" Model: Model of decision making that states that organizations are not rational and that decisions are solutions that become attached to problems for accidental reasons.

General Controls: Overall controls that establish a framework for controlling the design, security, and use of computer programs throughout an organization.

Genetic Algorithms: Problem-solving methods that promote the evolution of solutions to specified problems using the model of living organisms adapting to their environment.

Geographic Information System (GIS): System with software that can analyze and display data using digitized maps to enhance planning and decision-making.

Graphical User Interface (GUI): The part of an operating system users interact with that uses graphic icons and the computer mouse to issue commands and make selections.

Grid Computing: Applying the resources of many computers in a network to a single problem.

Group Decision-Support System (GDSS): An interactive computer-based system to facilitate the solution to unstructured problems by a set of decision makers working together as a group.

Groupware: Software that provides functions and services that support the collaborative activities of work groups.

H

Hierarchical DBMS: One type of logical database model that organizes data in a treelike structure. A record is subdivided into segments that are connected to each other in one-to-many parent-child relationships.

High-Availability Computing: Tools and technologies ,including backup hardware resources, to enable a system to recover quickly from a crash.

Human Resources Information Systems: Systems that maintain employee records, track employee skills, job performance and training, and support planning for employee compensation and career development.

Hybrid AI Systems: Integration of multiple AI technologies into a single application to take advantage of the best features of these technologies.

Hypermedia Database: An approach to data management that organizes data as a network of nodes linked in any pattern the user specifies; the nodes can contain text, graphics, sound, full-motion video, or executable programs.

I

Immanuel Kant's Categorical Imperative: A principle that states that if an action is not right for everyone to take it is not right for anyone.

Implementation: Simon's final stage of decision-making, when the individual puts the decision into effect and reports on the progress of the solution.

Industry Structure: The nature of participants in an industry and their relative bargaining power. Derives from the competitive forces and establishes the general business environment in an industry and the overall profitability of doing business in that environment.

Inference Engine: The strategy used to search through the rule base in an expert system; can be forward or backward chaining.

Information: Data that have been shaped into a form that is meaningful and useful to human beings.

Information Appliance: Device that has been customized to perform a few specialized computing tasks well with minimal user effort.

Information Architecture: The particular design that information technology takes in a specific organization to achieve selected goals or functions.

Information Asymmetry: Situation where the relative bargaining power of two parties in a transaction is determined by one party in the transaction possessing more information essential to the transaction than the other party.

Information Center: A special facility within an organization that provides training and support for end-user computing.

Information Partnership: Cooperative alliance formed between two or more corporations for the purpose of sharing information to gain strategic advantage.

Information Policy: Formal rules governing the maintenance, distribution, and use of information in an organization.

Information Requirements: A detailed statement of the information needs that a new system must satisfy; identifies who needs what information, and when, where, and how the information is needed.

Information Rights: The rights that individuals and organizations have with respect to information that pertains to themselves.

Information System: Interrelated components working together to collect, process, store, and disseminate information to support decision making, coordination, control, analysis, and visualization in an organization.

Information Systems Department: The formal organizational unit that is responsible for the information systems function in the organization.

Information Systems Literacy: Broad-based understanding of information systems that includes behavioral knowledge about organizations and individuals using information systems as well as technical knowledge about computers.

Information Systems Managers: Leaders of the various specialists in the information systems department.

Information Systems Plan: A road map indicating the direction of systems development: the rationale, the current situation, the management strategy, the implementation plan, and the budget.

Information Technology (IT) Infrastructure: Computer hardware, software, data, storage technology, and networks providing a portfolio of shared IT resources for the organization.

Informational Roles: Mintzberg's classification for managerial roles where managers act as the nerve centers of their organizations, receiving and disseminating critical information.

Informed Consent: Consent given with knowledge of all the facts needed to make a rational decision.

Input: The capture or collection of raw data from within the organization or from its external environment for processing in an information system.

Input Controls: The procedures to check data for accuracy and completeness when they enter the system.

Instant Messaging: Chat service that allows participants to create their own private chat channels so that a person can be alerted whenever someone on his or her private list is on-line to initiate a chat session with that particular individual.

Intangible Benefits: Benefits that are not easily quantified; they include more efficient customer service or enhanced decision making.

Integrated Services Digital Network (ISDN): International standard for transmitting voice, video, image, and data to support a wide range of service over the public telephone lines.

Integrated Software Package: A software package that provides two or more applications, such as word processing and spreadsheets, providing for easy transfer of data between them.

Intellectual Property: Intangible property created by individuals or corporations that is subject to protections under trade secret, copyright, and patent law.

Intelligence: The first of Simon's four stages of decision making, when the individual collects information to identify problems occurring in the organization.

Intelligent Agent: Software program that uses a built-in or learned knowledge base to carry out specific, repetitive, and predictable tasks for an individual user, business process, or software application.

Internal Integration Tools: Project management technique that ensures that the implementation team operates as a cohesive unit.

Internal Rate of Return (IRR): The rate of return or profit that an investment is expected to earn.

Interorganizational Systems: Information systems that automate the flow of information across organizational boundaries and link a company to its customers, distributors, or suppliers.

Interpersonal Roles: Mintzberg's classification for managerial roles where managers act as figureheads and leaders for the organization.

Intrusion Detection System: Tools to monitor the most vulnerable points in a network to detect and deter unauthorized intruders.

Intuitive Decision Makers: Cognitive style that describes people who approach a problem with multiple methods in an unstructured manner, using trial and error to find a solution.

Investment Workstation: Powerful desktop computer for financial specialists, which is optimized to access and manipulate massive amounts of financial data.

Iteration Construct: The logic pattern in programming where certain actions are repeated while a specified condition occurs or until a certain condition is met.

Iterative: A process of repeating over and over again the steps to build a system.

J

Java: Programming language that can deliver only the software functionality needed for a particular task, such as a small applet downloaded from a network; can run on any computer and operating system.

Joint Application Design (JAD): Process to accelerate the generation of information requirements by having end users and information systems specialists work together in intensive interactive design sessions.

Just-In-Time: Scheduling system for minimizing inventory by having components arrive exactly at the moment they are needed and finished goods shipped as soon as they leave the assembly line.

K

Key Field: A field in a record that uniquely identifies instances of that record so that it can be retrieved, updated, or sorted.

Knowledge: Concepts, experience, and insight that provide a framework for creating, evaluating, and using information.

Knowledge- and Information-Intense Products: Products that require a great deal of learning and knowledge to produce.

Knowledge Base: Model of human knowledge that is used by expert systems.

Knowledge Discovery: Identification of novel and valuable patterns in large databases.

Knowledge Engineer: A specialist who elicits information and expertise from other professionals and translates it into a set of rules, or frames, for an expert system.

Knowledge Management: The set of processes developed in an organization to create, gather, store, maintain, and disseminate the firm's knowledge.

Knowledge Management Systems: Systems that support the creation, capture, storage, and dissemination of firm expertise and knowledge.

Knowledge Network: Online directory for locating corporate experts in well-defined knowledge domains.

Knowledge Repository: Collection of documented internal and external knowledge in a single location for more efficient management and utilization by the organization.

Knowledge Workers: People such as engineers or architects who design products or services and create knowledge for the organization.

L

Learning Management System (LMS): Tools for the management, delivery, tracking, and assessment of various types of employee learning.

Legacy System: A system that has been in existence for a long time and that continues to be used to avoid the high cost of replacing or redesigning it.

Liability: The existence of laws that permit individuals to recover the damages done to them by other actors, systems, or organizations.

Load Balancing: Distribution of large numbers of requests for access among multiple servers so that no single device is overwhelmed.

Logistics: Planning and control of all factors that will have an impact on transporting a product or service.

M

Machine Cycle: Series of operations required to process a single machine instruction.

Machine Language: A programming language consisting of the 1s and 0s of binary code.

Magnetic Disk: A secondary storage medium in which data are stored by means of magnetized spots on a hard or floppy disk.

Magnetic Tape: Inexpensive, older secondary-storage medium in which large volumes of information are stored sequentially by means of magnetized and nonmagnetized spots on tape.

Mainframe: Largest category of computer, used for major business processing.

Maintenance: Changes in hardware, software, documentation, or procedures to a production system to correct errors, meet new requirements, or improve processing efficiency.

Managed Security Service Provider (MSSP): Company that provides security management services for subscribing clients.

Management Control: Monitoring how efficiently or effectively resources are utilized and how well operational units are performing.

Management Information Systems (MIS): The study of information systems focusing on their use in business and management..

Management-Level Systems: Information systems that support the monitoring, controlling, decision-making, and administrative activities of middle managers.

Managerial Roles: Expectations of the activities that managers should perform in an organization.

Man-Month: The traditional unit of measurement used by systems designers to estimate the length of time to complete a project. Refers to the amount of work a person can be expected to complete in a month.

Manufacturing and Production Information Systems: Systems that deal with the planning, development, and production of products and services and with controlling the flow of production.

Market Segmentation: Dividing a heterogeneous market into smaller, more homogeneous subgroups where marketing efforts can be more specifically targeted and effective.

Mass Customization: The capacity to offer individually tailored products or services using mass production resources..

Massively Parallel Computers: Computers that use hundreds or thousands of processing chips to attack large computing problems simultaneously.

Megahertz: A measure of cycle speed, or the pacing of events in a computer; one megahertz equals one million cycles per second.

Message Integrity: The ability to ascertain that a transmitted message has not been copied or altered.

Metric: A standard measurement of performance.

Metropolitan Area Network (MAN): Network that spans a metropolitan area, usually a city and its major suburbs. Its geographic scope falls between a WAN and a LAN.

Micropayment: Payment for a very small sum of money, often less than $10.

Middle Managers: People in the middle of the organizational hierarchy who are responsible for carrying out the plans and goals of senior management.

Middleware: Software that connects two disparate applications, allowing them to communicate with each other and to exchange data.

Mirroring: Duplicating all the processes and transactions of a server on a backup server to prevent any interruption in service if the primary server fails.

MIS Audit: Identifies all the controls that govern individual information systems and assesses their effectiveness.

m-Commerce: The use of wireless devices, such as cell phones or handheld digital information appliances, to conduct both business-to-consumer and business-to-business e-commerce transactions over the Internet.

Mobile Data Networks: Wireless networks that enable two-way transmission of data files cheaply and efficiently.

Model: An abstract representation that illustrates the components or relationships of a phenomenon.

Model-Driven DSS: Primarily stand-alone system that uses some type of model to perform "what-if" and other kinds of analyses.

Module: A logical unit of a program that performs one or several functions.

Multicasting: Transmission of data to a selected group of recipients.

Multinational: Form of business organization that concentrates financial management and control out of a central home base while decentralizing

Multiplexing: Ability of a single communications channel to carry data transmissions from multiple sources simultaneously.

N

Natural Language: Nonprocedural language that enables users to communicate with the computer using conversational commands resembling human speech.

Net Marketplace: A single digital marketplace based on Internet technology linking many buyers to many sellers.

Net Present Value (NPV): The amount of money an investment is worth, taking into account its cost, earnings, and the time value of money.

Network: The linking of two or more computers to share data or resources, such as a printer.

Network Economics: Model of strategic systems at the industry level based on the concept of a network where adding another participant entails zero marginal costs but can create much larger marginal gains.

Network Operating System (NOS): Special software that routes and manages communications on the network and coordinates network resources.

Neural Network: Hardware or software that attempts to emulate the processing patterns of the biological brain.

Nomadic Computing: Wireless computing where users move from wireless hot spot to wireless hot spot to gain network or Internet access.

Nonobvious Relationship Awareness (NORA): Technology that can find obscure hidden connections between people or other entities by analyzing information from many different sources to correlate relationships.

Normalization: The process of creating small stable data structures from complex groups of data when designing a relational database.

O

Object-Oriented DBMS: An approach to data management that stores both data and the procedures acting on the data as objects that can be automatically retrieved and shared; the objects can contain multimedia.

Object-Oriented Development: Approach to systems development that uses the object as the basic unit of systems analysis and design. The system is modeled as a collection o objects and the relationship between them.

Object-Oriented Programming: An approach to software development that combines data and procedures into a single object.

Object-Relational DBMS: A database management system that combines the capabilities of a relational DBMS for storing traditional information and the capabilities of an object-oriented DBMS for storing graphics and multimedia.

Office Systems: Systems such as word processing, desktop publishing, e-mail, electronic scheduling, and videoconferencing, designed to increase worker productivity in the office.

On-Line Transaction Processing: Transaction processing mode in which transactions entered on-line are immediately processed by the computer.

Open Systems Interconnect (OSI): Less widely used network connectivity model developed by International Standards Organization for linking different types of computers and networks.

Open-Source Software: Software that provides free access to its program code, allowing users to modify the program code to make improvements or fix errors.

Operational Control: Deciding how to carry out specific tasks specified by upper and middle management and establishing criteria for completion and resource allocation.

Operational CRM: Customer-facing applications, such as sales force automation, call center and customer service support, and marketing automation.

Operational Managers: People who monitor the day-to-day activities of the organization.

Operational-Level Systems: Information systems that monitor the elementary activities and transactions of the organization.

Opt-In: Model of informed consent permitting prohibiting an organization from collecting any personal information unless the individual specifically takes action to approve information collection and use.

Opt-Out: Model of informed consent permitting the collection of personal information until the consumer specifically requests that the data not be collected.

Optical Network: High-speed networking technologies for transmitting data in the form of light pulses.

Organization (behavioral definition): A collection of rights, privileges, obligations, and responsibilities that are delicately balanced over a period of time through conflict and conflict resolution.

Organization (technical definition): A stable, formal, social structure that takes resources from the environment and processes them to produce outputs.

Organizational And Management Capital: Investments in organization and management such as new business processes, management behavior, organizational culture, or training.

Organizational Culture: The set of fundamental assumptions about what products the organization should produce, how and where it should produce them, and for whom they should be produced.

Organizational Impact Analysis: Study of the way a proposed system will affect organizational structure, attitudes, decision making, and operations.

Organizational Learning: Creation of new standard operating procedures and business processes that reflect organizations' experience.

Organizational Memory: The stored learning from an organization's history that can be used for decision making and other purposes.

Organizational Models Of Decision Making: Models of decision making that take into account the structural and political characteristics of an organization.

Output Controls: Measures that ensure that the results of computer processing are accurate, complete, and properly distributed.

Output: The distribution of processed information to the people who will use it or to the activities for which it will be used.

Outsourcing: The practice of contracting computer center operations, telecommunications networks, or applications development to external vendors.

P

P3P: Industry standard designed to give users more control over personal information gathered on Web sites they visit. Stands for Platform for Privacy Preferences Project.

Packet Switching: Technology that breaks messages into small, fixed bundles of data and routes them in the most economical way through any available communications channel..

Paging System: A wireless transmission technology in which the pager beeps when the user receives a message; used to transmit short alphanumeric messages.

Paradigm Shift: Radical reconceptualization of the nature of the business and the nature of the organization.

Parallel Processing: Type of processing in which more than one instruction can be processed at a time by breaking down a problem into smaller parts and processing them simultaneously with multiple processors.

Parallel Strategy: A safe and conservative conversion approach where both the old system and its potential replacement are run together for a time until everyone is assured that the new one functions correctly.

Partner Relationship Management (PRM): Automation of the firm's relationships with its selling partners using customer data and analytical tools to improve coordination and customer sales.

Payback Method: A measure of the time required to pay back the initial investment on a project.

Peer-To-Peer Computing: Form of distributed processing that links computers via the Internet or private networks so that they can share processing tasks.

Peer-To-Peer Payment System: Electronic payment system for people who want to send money to vendors or individuals who are not set up to accept credit card payments.

Peer-To-Peer: Network architecture that gives equal power to all computers on the network; used primarily in small networks.

Phased Approach: Introduces the new system in stages either by functions or by organizational units.

Pilot Study: A strategy to introduce the new system to a limited area of the organization until it is proven to be fully functional; only then can the conversion to the new system across the entire organization take place.

Political Models Of Decision Making: Models of decision making where decisions result from competition and bargaining among the organization's interest groups and key leaders.

Pop-Up Ad: Ad that opens automatically and does not disappear until the user clicks on it.

Portfolio Analysis: An analysis of the portfolio of potential applications within a firm to determine the risks and benefits, and to select among alternatives for information systems.

Post-Implementation Audit: Formal review process conducted after a system has been placed in production to determine how well the system has met its original objectives.

Predictive Analysis: Use of datamining techniques, historical data, and assumptions about future conditions to predict outcomes of events.

Present Value: The value, in current dollars, of a payment or stream of payments to be received in the future.

Primary Activities: Activities most directly related to the production and distribution of a firm's products or services.

Primary Storage: Part of the computer that temporarily stores program instructions and data being used by the instructions.

Privacy: The claim of individuals to be left alone, free from surveillance or interference from other individuals, organizations, or the state.

Private Exchange: Web-enabled networks linking systems of multiple firms in an industry for the coordination of trans-organizational business processes.

Process Specifications: Describe the logic of the processes occurring within the lowest levels of a data flow diagram.

Processing Controls: The routines for establishing that data are complete and accurate during updating.

Processing: The conversion, manipulation, and analysis of raw input into a form that is more meaningful to humans.

Procurement: Sourcing goods and materials, negotiating with suppliers, paying for goods, and making delivery arrangements.

Product Differentiation: Competitive strategy for creating brand loyalty by developing new and unique products and services that are not easily duplicated by competitors.

Production Or Service Workers: People who actually produce the products or services of the organization.

Production: The stage after the new system is installed and the conversion is complete; during this time the system is reviewed by users and technical specialists to determine how well it has met its original goals.

Profiling: The use of computers to combine data from multiple sources and create electronic dossiers of detailed information on individuals.

Profitability Index: Used to compare the profitability of alternative investments; it is calculated by dividing the present value of the total cash inflow from an investment by the initial cost of the investment.

Program-Data Dependence: The close relationship between data stored in files and the software programs that update and maintain those files. Any change in data organization or format requires a change in all the programs associated with those files.

Protocol: A set of rules and procedures that govern transmission between the components in a network.

Prototype: The preliminary working version of an information system for demonstration and evaluation purposes.

Prototyping: The process of building an experimental system quickly and inexpensively for demonstration and evaluation so that users can better determine information requirements.

Public Key Infrastructure: System for creating public and private keys using a certificate authority (CA) and digital certificates for authentication.

Pull-Based Model: Supply chain driven by actual customer orders or purchases so that members of the supply chain produce and deliver only what customers have ordered.

Pure-Play: Business models based purely on the Internet.

Push-Based Model: Supply chain driven by production master schedules based on forecasts or best guesses of demand for products, and products are "pushed" to customers.

"Push" Technology: Method of obtaining relevant information on networks by having a computer broadcast information directly to the user based on prespecified interests.

Q/R

Query Language: Software tool that provides immediate online answers to requests for information that are not predefined.

Radio-Frequency Identification (RFID): Technology using tiny tags with embedded microchips containing data about an item and its location to transmit short-distance radio signals to special RFID readers that then pass the data on to a computer for processing.

RAID (Redundant Array of Inexpensive Disks): Disk storage technology to boost disk performance by packaging more than 100 smaller disk drives with a controller chip and specialized software in a single large unit to deliver data over multiple paths simultaneously.

RAM (Random Access Memory): Primary storage of data or program instructions that can directly access any randomly chosen location in the same amount of time.

Rapid Application Development (RAD): Process for developing systems in a very short time period by using prototyping, fourth-generation tools, and close teamwork among users and systems specialists.

Rational Model: Model of human behavior based on the belief that people, organizations, and nations engage in basically consistent, value-maximizing calculations.

Rationalization Of Procedures: The streamlining of standard operating procedures, eliminating obvious bottlenecks, so that automation makes operating procedures more efficient.

Reach: Measurement of how many people a business can connect with and how many products it can offer those people.

Real Options Pricing Models: Models for evaluating information technology investments with uncertain returns by using techniques for valuing financial options.

Record: A group of related fields.

Reduced Instruction Set Computing (RISC): Technology used to enhance the speed of microprocessors by embedding only the most frequently used instructions on a chip.

Reintermediation: The shifting of the intermediary role in a value chain to a new source.

Relational DBMS: A type of logical database model that treats data as if they were stored in two-dimensional tables. It can relate data stored in one table to data in another as long as the two tables share a common data element.

Repetitive Stress Injury (RSI): Occupational disease that occurs when muscle groups are forced through repetitive actions with high-impact loads or thousands of repetitions with low-impact loads.

Request for Proposal (RFP): A detailed list of questions submitted to vendors of software or other services to determine how well the vendor's product can meet the organization's specific requirements.

Resource Allocation: The determination of how costs, time, and personnel are assigned to different phases of a systems development project.

Responsibility: Accepting the potential costs, duties, and obligations for the decisions one makes.

Reverse Logistics: The return of items from buyers to sellers in a supply chain.

Richness: Measurement of the depth and detail of information that a business can supply to the customer as well as information the business collects about the customer.

Ring Network: A network topology in which all computers are linked by a closed loop in a manner that passes data in one direction from one computer to another.

Risk Assessment: Determining the potential frequency of the occurrence of a problem and the potential damage if the problem were to occur. Used to determine the cost/benefit of a control.

Risk Aversion Principle: Principle that one should take the action that produces the least harm or incurs the least cost.

Rule Base: The collection of knowledge in an AI system that is represented in the form of IF-THEN rules.

S

Safe Harbor: Private self-regulating policy and enforcement mechanism that meets the objectives of government regulations but does not involve government regulation or enforcement.

Sales and Marketing Information Systems: Systems that help the firm identify customers for the firm's products or services, develop products and services to meet their needs, promote these products and services, sell the products and services, and provide ongoing customer support.

Satellite: The transmission of data using orbiting satellites that serve as relay stations for transmitting microwave signals over very long distances.

Scalability: The ability of a computer, product, or system to expand to serve a larger number of users without breaking down.

Scoring Model: A quick method for deciding among alternative systems based on a system of ratings for selected objectives.

Search-Based Advertising: Payment to a search service to display a sponsored link to a company's Web site as a way of advertising that company.

Search Costs: The time and money spent locating a suitable product and determining the best price for that product.

Security: Policies, procedures, and technical measures used to prevent unauthorized access, alteration, theft, or physical damage to information systems.

Selection Construct: The logic pattern in programming where a stated condition determines which of two alternative actions can be taken.

Semantic Web: Collaborative effort led by the World Wide Web Consortium to make Web searching more efficient by reducing the amount of human involvement in searching for and processing web information.

Semistructured Knowledge: Information in the form of less structured objects, such as e-mail, chat room exchanges, videos, graphics, brochures, or bulletin boards.

Semistructured Knowledge System: System for organizing and storing less structured information, such as e-mail, voice mail, videos, graphics, brochures, or bulleting boards. Also known as digital asset management system.

Senior Managers: People occupying the topmost hierarchy in an organization who are responsible for making long-range decisions.

Sensitivity Analysis: Models that ask "what-if" questions repeatedly to determine the impact of changes in one or more factors on the outcomes.

Sequence Construct: The sequential single steps or actions in the logic of a program that do not depend on the existence of any condition.

Service Platform: Integration of multiple applications from multiple business functions, business units, or business partners to deliver a seamless experience for the customer, employee, manager, or business partner.

Six Sigma: A specific measure of quality, representing 3.4 defects per million opportunities; used to designate a set of methodologies and techniques for improving quality and reducing costs.

SOAP (Simple Object Access Protocol): Set of rules that allows Web services applications to pass data and instructions to one another.

Social Engineering: Tricking people into revealing their passwords by pretending to be legitimate users or members of a company in need of information.

Sociotechnical Design: Design to produce information systems that blend technical efficiency with sensitivity to organizational and human needs.

Software Metrics: The objective assessments of the software used in a system in the form of quantified measurements.

Spreadsheet: Software displaying data in a grid of columns and rows, with the capability of easily recalculating numerical data.

Standard Operating Procedures (SOPS): Formal rules for accomplishing tasks that have been developed to cope with expected situations.

Star Network: A network topology in which all computers and other devices are connected to a central host computer. All communications between network devices must pass through the host computer.

Storage Area Network (SAN): A high-speed network dedicated to storage that connects different kinds of storage devices, such as tape libraries and disk arrays so they can be shared by multiple servers.

Storage Service Provider (SSP): Third-party provider that rents out storage space to subscribers over the Web, allowing customers to store and access their data without having to purchase and maintain their own storage technology.

Storage Technology: Physical media and software governing the storage and organization of data for use in an information system.

Stored Value Payment Systems: Systems enabling consumers to make instant on-line payments to merchants and other individuals based on value stored in a digital account.

Strategic Decision Making: Determining the long-term objectives, resources, and policies of an organization.

Strategic Information Systems: Computer systems at any level of the organization that change goals, operations, products, services, or environmental relationships to help the organization gain a competitive advantage.

Strategic Transitions: A movement from one level of sociotechnical system to another. Often required when adopting strategic systems that demand changes in the social and technical elements of an organization.

Strategic-Level Systems: Information systems that support the long-range planning activities of senior management.

Streaming Technology: Technology for transferring data so that they can be processed as a steady and continuous stream.

Structure Chart: System documentation showing each level of design, the relationship among the levels, and the overall place in the design structure; can document one program, one system, or part of one program.

Structured: Refers to the fact that techniques are carefully drawn up, step by step, with each step building on a previous one.

Structured Analysis: A method for defining system inputs, processes, and outputs and for partitioning systems into subsystems or modules that show a logical graphic model of information flow.

Structured Decisions: Decisions that are repetitive, routine, and have a definite procedure for handling them.

Structured Design: Software design discipline encompassing a set of design rules and techniques for designing systems from the top down in hierarchical fashion.

Structured Knowledge: Knowledge in the form of structured documents and reports.

structured knowledge system: System for organizing structured knowledge in a repository where it can be accessed throughout the organization. Also known as content management system.

Structured Programming: Discipline for organizing and coding programs that simplifies the control paths so that the programs can be easily understood and modified; uses the basic control structures and modules that have only one entry point and one exit point.

Structured Query Language (SQL): The standard data manipulation language for relational database management systems.

Subschema: The specific set of data from the database that is required by each user or application program.

Supercomputer: Highly sophisticated and powerful computer that can perform very complex computations extremely rapidly.

Supply Chain: Network of organizations and business processes for procuring materials, transforming raw materials into intermediate and finished products, and distributing the finished products to customers.

Supply Chain Execution Systems: Systems to manage the flow of products through distribution centers and warehouses to ensure that products are delivered to the right locations in the most efficient manner.

Supply Chain Management: Integration of supplier, distributor, and customer logistics requirements into one cohesive process.

Supply Chain Management Systems: Information systems that automate the flow of information between a firm and its suppliers in order to optimize the planning, sourcing, manufacturing, and delivery of products and services.

Supply Chain Planning Systems: Systems that enable a firm to generate demand forecasts for a product and to develop sourcing and manufacturing plans for that product.

Support Activities: Activities that make the delivery of a firm's primary activities possible. Consist of the organization's infrastructure, human resources, technology, and procurement.

Switched Lines: Telephone lines that a person can access from a terminal to transmit data to another computer, the call being routed or switched through paths to the designated destination.

Switching Costs: The expense a customer or company incurs in lost time and expenditure of resources when changing from one supplier or system to a competing supplier or system.

Syndicator: Business aggregating content or applications from multiple sources, packaging them for distribution, and reselling them to third-party Web sites.

System Failure: An information system that either does not perform as expected, is not operational at a specified time, or cannot be used in the way it was intended.

System Software: Generalized programs that manage the computer's resources, such as the central processor, communications links, and peripheral devices.

System Testing: Tests the functioning of the information system as a whole in order to determine if discrete modules will function together as planned.

Systematic Decision Makers: Cognitive style that describes people who approach a problem by structuring it in terms of some formal method.

Systems Analysis: The analysis of a problem that the organization will try to solve with an information system.

Systems Analysts: Specialists who translate business problems and requirements into information requirements and systems, acting as liaison between the information systems department and the rest of the organization.

Systems Design: Details how a system will meet the information requirements as determined by the systems analysis.

Systems Development: The activities that go into producing an information systems solution to an organizational problem or opportunity.

Systems Lifecycle: A traditional methodology for developing an information system that partitions the systems development process into formal stages that must be completed sequentially with a very formal division of labor between end users and information systems specialists.

T

Tacit Knowledge: Expertise and experience of organizational members that has not been formally documented.

Tangible Benefits: Benefits that can be quantified and assigned a monetary value; they include lower operational costs and increased cash flows.

Taxonomy: Method of classifying things according to a predetermined system.

Teamware: Group collaboration software that is customized for teamwork.

Technostress: Stress induced by computer use; symptoms include aggravation, hostility toward humans, impatience, and enervation.

Test Plan: Prepared by the development team in conjunction with the users; it includes all of the preparations for the series of tests to be performed on the system.

Testing: The exhaustive and thorough process that determines whether the system produces the desired results under known conditions.

Touch Point: Method of firm interaction with a customer, such as telephone, e-mail, customer service desk, conventional mail, or point-of-purchase.

Topology: The way in which the components of a network are connected.

Total Cost of Ownership (TCO): Designates the total cost of owning technology resources, including initial purchase costs, the cost of hardware and software upgrades, maintenance, technical support, and training.

Total Quality Management (TQM): A concept that makes quality control a responsibility to be shared by all people in an organization.

Trade Secret: Any intellectual work or product used for a business purpose that can be classified as belonging to that business, provided it is not based on information in the public domain.

Transaction Cost Theory: Economic theory stating that firms grow larger because they can conduct marketplace transactions internally more cheaply than they can with external firms in the marketplace.

Transaction Processing Systems (TPS): Computerized systems that perform and record the daily routine transactions necessary to conduct the business; they serve the organization's operational level.

Transborder Data Flow: The movement of information across international boundaries in any form.

Transmission Control Protocol/Internet Protocol (TCP/IP): Dominant model for achieving connectivity among different networks. Provides a universally agree-on method for breaking up digital messages into packets, routing them to the proper addresses, and then reassembling them into coherent messages.

Transnational: Truly global form of business organization with no national headquarters; value-added activities are managed from a global perspective without reference to national borders, optimizing sources of supply and demand and local competitive advantage.

tuple: A row or record in a relational database.

U

UDDI (Universal Description, Discovery, and Integration): Allows a Web service to be listed in a directory of Web services so that it can be easily located by other organizations and systems.

Unified Modeling Language (UML): Industry standard methodology for analysis and design of an object-oriented software system.

Uniform Resource Locator (URL): The address of a specific resource on the Internet.

unit testing: The process of testing each program separately in the system. Sometimes called program testing.

UNIX: Operating system for all types of computers, which is machine independent and supports multiuser processing, multitasking, and networking. Used in high-end workstations and servers.

Unstructured Decisions: Nonroutine decisions in which the decision maker must provide judgment, evaluation, and insights into the problem definition; there is no agreed-upon procedure for making such decisions.

Up-Selling: Marketing higher-value products or services to new or existing customers.

Usenet: Forums in which people share information and ideas on a defined topic through large electronic bulletin boards where anyone can post messages on the topic for others to see and to which others can respond.

User Interface: The part of the information system through which the end user interacts with the system; type of hardware and the series of on-screen commands and responses required for a user to work with the system.

User-Designer Communications Gap: The difference in backgrounds, interests, and priorities that impede communication and problem solving among end users and information systems specialists.

Utilitarian Principle: Principle that assumes one can put values in rank order and understand the consequences of various courses of action.

V

Value Chain Model: Model that highlights the primary or support activities that add a margin of value to a firm's products or services where information systems can best be applied to achieve a competitive advantage.

Value Web: Customer-driven network of independent firms who use information technology to coordinate their value chains to collectively produce a product or service for a market.

Value-Added Network (VAN): Private, multipath, data-only, third-party-managed network that multiple organizations use on a subscription basis.

Virtual Organization: Organization using networks to link people, assets and ideas to create and distribute products and services without being limited to traditional organizational boundaries or physical location.

Virtual Private Network (VPN): A secure connection between two points across the Internet to transmit corporate data. Provides a low-cost alternative to a private network.

Virtual Reality Modeling Language (VRML): A set of specifications for interactive three-dimensional modeling on the World Wide Web.

Virtual Reality Systems: Interactive graphics software and hardware that create computer-generated simulations that provide sensations that emulate real-world activities.

Visual Programming: The construction of software programs by selecting and arranging programming objects rather than by writing program code.

W

Walkthrough: A review of a specification or design document by a small group of people carefully selected based on the skills needed for the particular objectives being tested.

Wide Area Network (WAN): Telecommunications network that spans a large geographical distance. May consist of a variety of cable, satellite, and microwave technologies.

Wireless Application Protocol (WAP): System of protocols and technologies that lets cell phones and other wireless devices with tiny displays, low-bandwidth connections, and minimal memory access Web-based information and services.

Wisdom: The collective and individual experience of applying knowledge to the solution of problems.

WML (Wireless Markup Language): Markup language for Wireless Web sites; based on XML and optimized for tiny displays.

Work-Flow Management: The process of streamlining business procedures so that documents can be moved easily and efficiently from one location to another.

WSDL (Web Services Description Language): Common framework for describing the tasks performed by a Web service so that it can be used by other applications.

BIBLIOGRAPHY

Ailawadi, K. L., Zhang, J., Krishna, A., & Kruger, M. W. (2010). When Wal-Mart enters: How incumbent retailers react and how this affects their sales outcomes. Journal of Marketing Research, 47(4), 577-593.

Asten, R. (1995). A virtual tug-of-war. Computer Reseller News, 5(29), 33-39.

Babcock, C. (2003, September). Amazon makes online merchandising easier. Information Week, 2 pages.

Bacheldor, B. (2004, March). From scratch: Amazon keeps supply chain close to home. Information Week, 1 page.

Bainbridge, E., Bevans, S., Keeley, B., & Oriel, K. (2011). The effects of the Nintendo Wii Fit on community-dwelling older adults with perceived balance deficits: A pilot study. Physical & Occupational Therapy in Geriatrics, 29(2), 126-135.

Benbasat, I., Goldstein, D. K., & Mead, M. (1987). The case research strategy in studies of information systems. MIS quarterly, 369-386.

Bettenhausen, S. (2007). Seasons BEATINGS. Electronic Gaming Monthly, 16(2), 34-36.

Brandt, R. (2011). One click: Jeff Bezos and the rise of Amazon.com. Penguin.

Carlton, J. (1995). Nintendo, video-game retailers discover treasure trove in Donkey Kong country. The Wall Street Journal, January 11, 1995, B1, B8.

Carlton, J. (1995). Nintendo, gambling with its technology, faces a crucial delay. The Wall Street Journal, May 5, 1995, A1, A4.

Chawla, S. (2011). Spanish police seize man for blackmailing Nintendo. Spinport News. February 16, 2011. Retrieved from http://spinport.com/spanish-police-seize-man-for-blackmailing-nintendo/314990/

Chevalier, J., & Goolsbee, A. (2003). Measuring prices and price competition online: Amazon. com and BarnesandNoble. com. Quantitative marketing and Economics, 1(2), 203-222.

Claburn, T. (2004, May). Amazon.com and Toys 'R' Us are on the outs. Information Week, 2 pages.

Claburn, T. (2004, June). Why Amazon is suing Toys 'R' Us. Information Week, 1 page.

Clark, R. A., Bryant, A. L., Pua, Y., McCrory, P., Bennell, K., & Hunt, M. (2010). Validity and reliability of the Nintendo Wii Balance Board for assessment of standing balance. Gait & posture, 31(3), 307-310.

CNN Online, "Wii Demand Still Outpaces Supply," July 2, 2007.

CNN Online, "Wii Could Top Record-Holding PS2," July 13, 2007.

Collett, D. (2002). Modelling binary data. CRC press.

Collett, S. (2002). The Web's best-seller. Computerworld, 30(9), 21-25.

Data Monitor, "Sony and Microsoft Case Studies," March 2004, p. 1-16.

DeJong, J. & Rash, W. (1992). Video madness. Corporate Computer, 1(2), 134- 144.

Evans, J. (2011). Will the Apple iPhone 5 kill Nintendo? Computerworld, August 11, 2011. Retrieved from http://blogs.computerworld.com/18781/will_the_apple_iphone_5_kill_nintendo

Fayyad, U. M., Piatetsky-Shapiro, G., Smyth, P., & Uthurusamy, R. (1996). Advances in knowledge discovery and data mining.

Gallagher, D. (2009). Sony drops PlayStation 3 price by $100. The Wall Street Journal, August 18, 2009, F6-F7. Gaudiosi, J. (2004). Game biz to enter a rollercoaster period. Video Store, 26(13), 144.

Geyskens, I., Gielens, K., & Dekimpe, M. G. (2002). The market valuation of internet channel additions. Journal of marketing, 66(2), 102-119.

Goodridge, E. & Nelson, M. (2000, May). Update: Amazon drops Sun, Compaq for HP. Information Week, May 31, 2000.

Gralla, P. (2006). Computing in the cloud. Computerworld, December 21, 2006.

Hansell, S. (2001). A front-row seat as Amazon gets serious. The New York Times, May 20, 2001, B2-B3.

Hayes, M. (2002, November). CDs, high heels, flannel shirts. Information Week, 2 pages.

Heun, C. (2001, March). What the rest of us can learn from Amazon. Information Week, 2 pages.

Heun, C. (2001, April). Amazon, borders team for superior customer service. Information Week, 2 pages.

Heun, C. (2001, July). Amazon Loss Shrinks; AOL Buys Amazon Search Service. Information Week, 2 pages.

Heun, C. (2001, August). Amazon Plugs into Circuit City in Profitability Drive. Information Week, August 27, 2001.

Johnson, R. (1993). The player: Nintendo is a force to reckon with - but not in interactive video. Computer Letter, 9(20), 6-9.

King, W. R. (2015). Planning for information systems. Routledge.

Konicki, S. (2000, October). Amazon taps Excelon to redo supply-chain system. Information Week, 2 pages.

Kontzer, T. (2001, September). Amazon teams with Expedia on online travel store," Information Week, 2 pages.

Leder, R. S., Azcarate, G., Savage, R., Savage, S., Sucar, L. E., Reinkensmeyer, D., ... & Molina, A. (2008, August). Nintendo Wii remote for computer simulated arm and wrist therapy in stroke survivors with upper extremity hemipariesis. In Virtual Rehabilitation, 2008 (pp. 74-74). IEEE.

Letzing, J. (2011). Amazon wins reprieve on California tax in exchange for jobs. The Wall Street Journal, September 23, 2011, B3-B5.

Linden, G., Smith, B., & York, J. (2003). Amazon.com recommendations: Item-to-item collaborative filtering. Internet Computing, IEEE, 7(1), 76-80.

Mangalindan, M. (2005). Threatening eBay's dominance, more online sellers go it alone. The Wall Street Journal, June 22, 2005, A21, A25.

Markoff, J. (2011). Software out there. The New York Times, April 5, 2006, B13.

Murphy, C. (2003, June). Amazon, the services firm. Information Week, 2 pages.

Peers, M. (2011). Launching new tablet, Amazon plays with Fire. The Wall Street Journal, September 29, 2011, B8.

Pratt, M. (2011). Feds Race to the Cloud. Computerworld, July 13, 2011.

Tibken, S. (2011). Amazon cloud snafu disrupts Websites. The Wall Street Journal, April 21, 2011, B12-B13.

Vogels, W. (2007, September). Data access patterns in the Amazon.com technology platform. In Proceedings of the 33rd international conference on Very large data bases (pp. 1-1). VLDB

Endowment.

Whiting, R. (2002). System overhaul boosts Amazon's inventory update time. Information Week, February 19, 2002, 3 pages.

Woo, S. (2011). Expenses eat at Amazon's profit. The Wall Street Journal, January 28, 2011, F1-F4.

Woo, S. & Kung, M. (2011). Netflix, Amazon add to movies. The Wall Street Journal, September 27, 2011, F2-F4.

THOMAS L BUCK

ABOUT THE AUTHOR

Dr. Thomas Buck is a Professor / Lecturer in the School of Business and Technology, at the College of St. Scholastica of Duluth, MN and teaches courses in management ethics, technology ethics, ecommerce, information systems and programming. With a PhD specializing in Educational Technology, Information Systems and Assessment, and an MS in Curriculum and Instruction, Dr. Buck's work includes teaching, research, and antiques.

His research work is two-fold, (i) web-based assessment tools and educational game design; and, (ii) e-commerce and cultural entrepreneurship. In assessment tools and game design, he is conducting an on-going research project on learning styles and distance learning, focusing on the developmental principles of educational psychology, game design, gender role theory, and assessment. He has also published a number of peer reviewed studies and books on topics ranging from Learning Styles and Web-based Learning to Technology Literacy Recommendations for colleges and universities. His related published works include his book, Learning in Cyberspace: A Guide to Authentic Assessment Tools for Web-based Instruction, and his McGraw-Hill/Irwin 2014 Distinguished Papers Award winning paper, Living the Case Study: Teaching Management and Leadership Ethics Through Serious Games, published by The Society for the Advancement of Information Systems.

As a Cultural Entrepreneur and internationally recognized Conservator of East Asian Historical & Cultural Artifacts, another one of Dr. Buck's passions is his research on Japanese and Chinese history, philosophy and fine arts. Among his related published works are his books "The Art of Tsukamaki" and "Ancient Japanese Swords and Fittings", both available on Amazon.com.

THOMAS L BUCK

CPSIA information can be obtained
at www.ICGtesting.com
Printed in the USA
LVOW09s1321050417
529713LV00017B/323/P